SpringerBriefs in Computer Science

Series Editors
Stan Zdonik
Shashi Shekhar
Jonathan Katz
Xindong Wu
Lakhmi C. Jain
David Padua
Xuemin (Sherman) Shen
Borko Furht
V.S. Subrahmanian
Martial Hebert
Katsushi Ikeuchi
Bruno Siciliano
Sushil Jajodia
Newton Lee

More information about this series at http://www.springer.com/series/10028

Pär J. Ågerfalk • Brian Fitzgerald
Klaas-Jan Stol

Software Sourcing in the Age of Open

Leveraging the Unknown Workforce

Foreword by Matt Germonprez and Joseph Feller

 Springer

Pär J. Ågerfalk
Department of Informatics and Media
Uppsala University
Uppsala, Sweden

Brian Fitzgerald
Lero — the Irish Software
    Research Centre
University of Limerick
Limerick, Ireland

Klaas-Jan Stol
Lero — the Irish Software
    Research Centre
University of Limerick
Limerick, Ireland

ISSN 2191-5768   ISSN 2191-5776   (electronic)
SpringerBriefs in Computer Science
ISBN 978-3-319-17265-1   ISBN 978-3-319-17266-8   (eBook)
DOI 10.1007/978-3-319-17266-8

Library of Congress Control Number: 2015935558

Springer Cham Heidelberg New York Dordrecht London

Printed on acid-free paper

Springer International Publishing AG Switzerland is part of Springer Science+Business Media (www.springer.com)

Foreword

Academic researchers tend to be driven by a mix of wonder and skepticism, welling up in the form of constant, almost obsessive questioning—in particular questioning the underlying assumptions behind words and expressions. We suppose we are true to the breed, as we have structured this foreword by questioning two of the key assumptions implied by the title of the book, *Software Sourcing in the Age of Open*: *Leveraging the Unknown Workforce*. First:

Is This Actually the "Age of Open"?

In December 2014, we, along with 38 of our colleagues from around the world (including the book's authors), established SIGOPEN, a special interest group of the Association for Information Systems to serve the global community of "open" researchers. The formation of the SIG was a very long time in the making.

For over 15 years, a steadily and rapidly growing global community of researchers have been turning their attention toward an explosion of interconnected phenomena such as open source software, content, hardware, and design; open innovation and distributed problem solving and invention; and collective intelligence, action, and resources (the "wisdom," "power," and "wealth" of "crowds").

These phenomena have emerged as disruptive modes of global collaboration predicated on open legal, social, economic, and technological systems and architectures. We believe strongly that these many types of "openness" are driving some of the most important contemporary innovations in the technologies we use and in the ways in which we use them—as individuals, organizations, and societies. And, collectively, we believe they can be reasonably understood as heralds of "the age of open" (or at least of "the age of open collaboration").

They are also heralds of an age of new questions because open strategies, platforms, and processes—particularly in the context of software development—are bringing organizations into intense interactions with increasingly diverse groups of people. This brings us to the second question:

Are We Truly Dealing with an "Unknown Workforce"?

Maybe so. But if that is the case, it is a problem to be corrected. We believe that the developmental modes discussed in this book are inherently dependent on not only making sense of openness but also making sense of each other, whether our collaborators take the form of crowds, communities, or colleagues. This book gives us an essential foundation upon which to begin this sense-making.

Ågerfalk, Fitzgerald, and Stol provide a foundation to help unpack and disambiguate what it means to be open and distributed, to help build trusted ecosystems with mutual benefits for all participants, and to help diverse participants react and respond to evolving communal situations. The authors provide a language to capture the nuances that exist in a complex world of sourcing, remuneration, and motivation, and highlight the challenges that arise when we attempt to speak of *crowdsourcing*, *opensourcing*, or *innersourcing* in light of each other.

Crowd-, open-, and innersourcing are all disruptive paradigms, each accommodating the changing nature of corporate and communal work differently, and each requiring focused, context-dependent attention. Narratives that treat open and distributed engagement as having a global sameness—placing all open engagements under a universal umbrella—fail to understand the nuances that separate them. This book reminds us that it is not only within the global narratives of open engagement, but also within the nuanced differences, that we can find new theoretical perspectives, develop deep practical implications, and foster strong communal practices. The authors highlight precise points of open engagement and reveal them to be deeply embedded in complex social and material contexts.

While there has been significant work done in the articulation of opensourcing, crowdsourcing, and innersourcing, helping to identify what openness is and what it can mean for a diverse set of participants, the story is far from complete. As academics, practitioners, and community members, this book pushes us to refine our ways of thinking about and representing the age of openness, challenging us to dig deeper and more precisely on these complex and challenging issues. *Software Sourcing in the Age of Open*: *Leveraging the Unknown Workforce* is thus an excellent entry point from which to join this important conversation.

Omaha, NE, USA   Matt Germonprez
Cork, Ireland   Joseph Feller

Acknowledgments

We are grateful to all the people and organizations that were involved in the studies presented in this book. Special thanks to Bram Riemens for sharing his valuable insights into the PFSPD project. This research was supported by Swedish Council for Working Life and Social Research grant 2010-1358 (Management and organization of open practices), Enterprise Ireland, grant IR/2013/0021 to the ITEA2-SCALARE project, Science Foundation Ireland, grant 10/CE/I1855 to Lero—the Irish Software Engineering Research Centre, and the Irish Research Council New Foundations programme.

Contents

About the Authors

Pär J. Ågerfalk is full professor and holder of the Chair in Information Systems at Uppsala University, Sweden. He received his Ph.D. from Linköping University and has held full-time positions at Örebro University, University of Limerick, Jönköping International Business School, and Lero—The Irish Software Engineering Research Centre. His research on open source software, globally distributed and flexible software development, information systems development methodology, and conceptual modelling has appeared in a number of leading information systems and software engineering journals, including *MIS Quarterly*, *Communications of the ACM* and *Information and Software Technology*. He is currently a co-editor of the *European Journal of Information Systems* and Dean of the Swedish Research School of Management and Information Technology. Ågerfalk is a founding member of the Special Interest Group on Open Research and Practice (SIGOPEN).

Brian Fitzgerald is Chief Scientist at Lero—the Irish Software Research Centre. He also holds an endowed professorship, the Krehbiel Chair in Innovation in Business and Technology at the University of Limerick. He holds a Ph.D. from the University of London and his research interests lie primarily in software development, encompassing open source and inner source, crowdsourcing software development, agile and lean software development, and global software development. His publications include 14 books, and over 150 peer-reviewed articles in the leading international journals and conferences in both the Information Systems and Software Engineering fields, including *MIS Quarterly*, *Information Systems Research*, *IEEE Transactions on Software Engineering*, and *ACM Transactions on Software Engineering Methodology*. Fitzgerald is a founding member of the Special Interest Group on Open Research and Practice (SIGOPEN).

Klaas-Jan Stol is a research fellow with Lero—the Irish Software Research Centre. He holds a Ph.D. in software engineering from the University of Limerick. His research interests include contemporary software development methods and strategies, including Inner Source, Open Source, crowdsourcing, and agile and lean methods, as well as research methodology and theory building in software engineering. His work has been published in several journals and magazines including *ACM Transactions on Software Engineering and Methodology*, *IEEE Software*, and *Information and Software Technology* as well as numerous international conferences including the *International Conference on Software Engineering*. He was formerly an active contributor to an open source project. Stol is a founding member of the Special Interest Group on Open Research and Practice (SIGOPEN).

Chapter 1
Setting the Scene

1.1 Introduction

Outsourcing of the software development activity has been on the increase in recent years according to both US[1] and European[2] reports. However, in many cases outsourcing of software development, often referred to as global software engineering, has not delivered on its promise (e.g. Lings et al. 2007; Nakatsu and Iacovou 2009; Tiwana and Keil 2009; Ó Conchúir et al. 2009). The success of the open source software movement, which seems to overcome many of the challenges associated with global software engineering, has been an inspiration for a number of specific forms of software sourcing, including opensourcing (Ågerfalk and Fitzgerald 2008), innersourcing (Stol and Fitzgerald 2015) and crowdsourcing (Stol and Fitzgerald 2014a). By integrating the findings from these earlier studies, this book explores and compares these forms of *open source-inspired sourcing*. These novel approaches to software sourcing differ from traditional outsourcing in significant ways and little is known about how they can work in practice. Therefore, our goal is to provide research-based advice to managers and developers facing software sourcing decisions.

The conventional wisdom of software engineering suggests that given the inherent complexity of software, it should be developed using tightly co-ordinated, centralised teams, following a rigorous development process. In recent times, the open source phenomenon has attracted considerable attention as an agile, practice-led initiative that appears to address the three core aspects of the so-called 'software crisis': namely, high cost of development, long development time-scale and poor quality of final software product. In terms of development cost, open source products are usually freely available for public download. From the point of view of development time-scale, the collaborative, parallel efforts of globally-distributed co-developers has allowed many open source products to be developed much more

---

[1] IT Outsourcing Statistics (2102/2013).

[2] European IT Outsourcing Intelligence Report.

© The Author(s) 2015
P.J. Ågerfalk et al., *Software Sourcing in the Age of Open*, SpringerBriefs
in Computer Science, DOI 10.1007/978-3-319-17266-8_1

quickly than conventional software. Finally, in terms of quality, many open source products are recognized for their high standards of reliability, efficiency and robustness, and the open source phenomenon has produced several market leaders in their respective areas—Linux and Apache spring to mind. Indeed, these are known as 'category killers,' so called because their success removes any incentive to develop competing products. The open source model also seems to harness the most scarce resource of all—talented software developers, many of whom exhibit a long-standing commitment to their chosen projects. It is further suggested that the resulting peer review model helps ensure the quality of the software produced (Feller and Fitzgerald 2002).

Previous research has argued for the importance of studying both the customer and supplier side of the outsourcing relationship (Koh et al. 2004). Nevertheless, most research on outsourcing tend to adopt the perspective of the customer (Gonzalez et al. 2006; Lacity et al. 2010). Interestingly, research on open source has all too often focused inwards on investigating the characteristics of the development process and projects, that is on the supplier side of the relationship, and far less has been conducted on the customer side, in the sense of investigating the consequences of the open source phenomenon for organizations, for example. However, in the three specific forms of software sourcing discussed in this book, namely opensourcing, innersourcing and crowdsourcing, the distinction between customer and supplier, or *company* and *community* as it may be termed in an opensourcing context, is a very important aspect that needs to be taken into account.

Furthermore, these three forms of sourcing differ from conventional outsourcing on a number of aspects. For example, in the case of traditional outsourcing, innersourcing and crowdsourcing, the locus of control is firmly with the customer company, and the community/supplier motivation is largely extrinsic for these three categories. However, in the case of opensourcing the locus of control is firmly with the supplier community and the motivation is largely intrinsic. On the other hand, if we consider the nature of the community workforce, in the case of outsourcing, this cohort is well known and is chosen on the basis of certifiably proven past performance. They also typically have some narrow but deep knowledge that is less economical to leverage within the customer company. On the other hand, in the case of opensourcing and crowdsourcing, the community workforce is largely unknown but possesses broad and deep knowledge thereby affording an opportunity for greater innovation for the customer company.

We return to these issues in Chap. 5 after having presented case studies of each of the three forms of software sourcing.

1.2 Intended Audience

This book has been written with two broad audiences in mind. First, the content should be of interest to managers and software developers that are considering different sourcing options. By pointing out characteristics along with benefits and pitfalls of each approach, we aim to provide a more nuanced and informed basis for software sourcing decisions. Second, the coverage of the three forms of sourcing with examples from industrial cases should serve as a good source of knowledge for postgraduate students interested in contemporary software sourcing approaches.

1.3 Definitions and Basic Sourcing Terminology

Given the nascent state of research on open source-inspired software sourcing, there are no commonly agreed definitions of the various forms of sourcing that emerge. Based on our previous research into opensourcing (Ågerfalk and Fitzgerald 2008), innersourcing (Stol and Fitzgerald 2015) and crowdsourcing (Stol and Fitzgerald 2014a), we present definitions for each of these sourcing strategies here.

1.3.1 Opensourcing

In recent years, the open source software (OSS) development model has gained significant momentum and is now generally considered to be a viable approach also in commercial settings. Similar to outsourcing, and particularly offshore sourcing, the open source development model promises many advantages. These include reduced salary costs; reduced cycle time arising from 'follow-the-sun' software development; cross-site modularization of development work; access to a larger skilled developer pool; innovation and shared best practice; and closer proximity to customers (Carmel 1999, 2006; Herbsleb and Grinter 1999; Carmel and Agarwal 2001; Ebert and De Neve 2001; Carmel and Tjia 2005; Ó Conchúir et al. 2009). Given that the primary force driving offshore sourcing appears to be cost savings (Lacity et al. 2010), it is not surprising that companies chose to focus on the open source development model as a potentially even cheaper alternative, as there are significant cost savings associated with the open source model (Wheeler 2004). Carmel and Tjia (2005) have characterized offshore sourcing as 'outsourcing to a global workforce.' Opensourcing, on the other hand, can best be characterized as outsourcing to a global but largely unknown workforce of open source developers. We use the term opensourcing to refer to the use of the open source development model as a software sourcing strategy. Open source software may be defined as software released under the terms of a license that basically allows the licensee to use, modify and redistribute, either *gratis* or for a fee. Of particular interest, however, is the recent phenomenon of opensourcing as a software development model. Similar to outsourcing, the open source development model allows companies to 'subcontract' development activities to another party. Since anyone (in principle) can join any open source project, the development community can reasonably be assumed to be global (Millar et al. 2005). The global nature of contributions to open source projects has been confirmed in several studies. For example, Lakhani and

Wolf (2005) conducted a survey on a sample of almost 10,000 projects in SourceForge and found that 55 % of respondents were from outside North America. Ghosh (2005) conducted a large-scale survey of almost 3,000 developers from across a broad range of open source projects, and estimated that almost 86 % of open source developers were from outside North America. In a study which focused specifically on Linux developers, Dempsey et al. (2002) reported non-North American developers performing the majority of development. Robles et al. (2001) studied a number of popular open source projects and found that 62 % of developers were from outside North America. This latter study is particularly noteworthy in that the authors performed a series of exhaustive checks to identify the country of origin of contributors. The global nature of the collaborative development found in all these studies suggests that opensourcing is truly a global phenomenon that can effectively be understood as a distinct approach to global software engineering.

Notably opensourcing is not limited to releasing previously proprietary software under an open source license and nurturing a community around the product. This approach to opensourcing—as, for example, practiced by IONA Technologies who released their flagship product Artix as open source under the name Celtix—we refer to as the 'liberation' approach. The reverse of this approach is when a company evolves from an existing open source product, as exemplified by the MySQL database management system (subsequently acquired by Sun Microsystems and Oracle) and the JBoss J2EE application server (subsequently acquired by RedHat). The latter can be referred to as the 'commercialization' approach to opensourcing. In this book we focus on the liberation approach since this is the most relevant alternative to innersourcing and crowdsourcing in terms of management sourcing decisions.

Despite the apparent similarities, three central aspects of open source clearly distinguish opensourcing from traditional outsourcing. These are (1) mutuality and reciprocity, (2) lack of formal contracts and (3) an emphasis on individuals rather than organizations.

Mutuality and reciprocity are critical to the success of the open source development model and are effectively enshrined in open source development through the 'copyleft' terms found in many open source licenses which decree that software can be used, modified and redistributed provided subsequent modifications are made freely available to others. Also, development is accomplished through the fulfillment of *mutual* expectations with respect to the activities of coding, debugging, testing and documentation. One of the most significant threats for the open source movement has been suggested to be the 'free rider' phenomenon whereby someone profits from open source without *reciprocating*, which thus contravenes these values of reciprocity and fulfillment of mutual expectations (Von Hippel and Von Krogh 2003).

Much open source development is done in the absence of any legal employment contract for developers. Also, the norms of how development is conducted are both written and unwritten. Developers are expected to be familiar with written rules and coding norms, for example, before they attempt to contribute (Feller and Fitzgerald 2002). However, the unwritten rules must also be learned by developers over time.

New recruits to development ranks serve their apprenticeship in learning these unwritten rules and norms of expected behavior (Gorman 2004; Raymond 2001).

The signaling incentive identified by Lerner and Tirole (2002) as the basic motivation for developers to contribute to open source projects (i.e. a combination of *career concerns* and *ego gratification*) apply primarily at the level of the individual. Furthermore, since many open source developers are not affiliated with any formal organization, an individual level of analysis is to some extent required in any study of open source developers.

1.3.2   Innersourcing

Numerous software development methods have been proposed to guide organizations in their software development: from the traditional waterfall approach and the V-model to the more recent and highly popular agile methods. While these methods all aim at providing a systematic way to develop software, the emergence of successful open source projects has been remarkable, given the seeming absence of a predefined process—what Erdogmus (2009) provokingly called an antiprocess. Open source communities have produced a number of high-quality and highly successful products, including the so-called LAMP stack (consisting of Linux, Apache, MySQL, and PHP/Perl/Python), while defying traditional wisdom in software development (McConnell 1999). Furthermore, while distributed development has proven extremely problematic and challenging for organizations (Herbsleb and Grinter 1999), open source software development represents a successful exemplar of distributed development. Several authors have argued for drawing lessons from open source communities and transferring those best practices to commercial software development (O'Reilly 1999; Asundi 2001; Augustin et al. 2002; Mockus and Herbsleb 2002; Erenkrantz and Taylor 2003; Fitzgerald 2011; Rigby et al. 2012). The open source phenomenon has attracted significant attention from the research community seeking to understand how open source communities can achieve such success. The success of open source has also captured the attention of many organizations who strive to replicate similar successes using the same approach. This phenomenon of organizations leveraging open source development practices for their in-house software development is what we label 'inner source,' though different organizations have used a variety of terms to denote this (Stol et al. 2011).

Inner source is defined as the adoption of open source development practices within the confines of an organization (Stol et al. 2011). Whereas well-defined methods, such as the agile Scrum approach, have clearly defined tasks (e.g., Scrum meetings), artifacts (e.g., Sprint backlog), and roles (e.g., Scrum Master), this is not so much the case for inner source, although common open source development practices and roles can be identified. Rather than a well-defined methodology, we consider inner source to be more of a development philosophy, oriented towards the open collaboration principles of egalitarianism, meritocracy, and self-organization

(Riehle et al. 2009). Within innersource, a number of common open source development practices can be observed:

- Universal access to development artifacts (e.g. source code);
- Transparent fishbowl development environment;
- Peer-review through organization-wide scrutiny of contributions;
- Informal communication channels (e.g., mailing lists, chats);
- Self-selection of motivated contributors;
- Frequent releases and early feedback;
- "Around the clock" development.

Which of these practices that are adopted as part of an inner source initiative varies per organization as each implementation of inner source is tailored to the particular context of the adopting organization (Gaughan et al. 2009). Existing development methods within a company may be augmented with open source practices, such as those just listed. However, a key tenet of inner source is universal access to the development artifacts throughout an organization so that anyone within the organization can potentially participate.

In addition to common practices, a number of common roles can be identified. Inner source projects are often 'grassroots' movements, started by individuals, project teams, or departments (Riemens and van Zon 2006; Gurbani et al. 2006; Melian 2007). As such, the initiator typically assumes the role of a benevolent dictator (Raymond 2001; Gurbani et al. 2006). As some contributors become experts in parts of the project, they can be promoted to trusted lieutenants (Gurbani et al. 2006), and together with the benevolent dictator form a core team. Similar governance structures are commonly found in open source projects (Mockus et al. 2002). In inner source, however, additional roles may emerge. Gurbani et al. (2010), for instance, identified a number of roles in the core team at Alcatel-Lucent, each of which had a specific function in order to tailor the bazaar to a commercial software development context.

As a project matures, it may attract more attention and support from management. Once an inner source project has been recognized to have significant business value which is critical to the organization at large, additional funding may be made available for the core team to provide ongoing support and training to the customers of the project.

1.3.3 Crowdsourcing

Software engineering no longer takes place in small, isolated groups of co-located developers, all working for the same employer, but increasingly takes place across organizations and communities involving many people. There is an increasing trend towards globalization with a focus on collaborative methods and infrastructure (Boehm 2006). One emerging approach to getting work done is crowdsourcing, a sourcing strategy that has emerged since the 1990s (Greengard 2011). Driven by new Internet technologies, organizations can tap into a workforce consisting of anyone with an Internet connection. Customers, or requesters, can advertise chunks of work, or tasks, on a crowdsourcing platform, where suppliers (i.e., individual workers) select those tasks that match their interests and abilities (Hoffmann 2009).

Crowdsourcing has been adopted in a wide variety of domains, such as design and sales of T-shirts (Howe 2008) and pharmaceutical research and development (Lakhani and Panetta 2007) and there are numerous crowdsourcing platforms through which customers and suppliers can find each other (Doan et al. 2011). One of the best known crowdsourcing platforms is Amazon Mechanical Turk (AMT) (Ipeirotis 2010). On AMT, chunks of work are referred to as Human Intelligence Tasks (HIT) or micro-tasks. Typical micro-tasks can be characterized as self-contained, simple, repetitive, short, and requiring little time, cognitive effort and specialized skills. Crowdsourcing has worked particularly well for such tasks (Kittur et al. 2011). Examples include tagging images, and translating fragments of text. As a result, remuneration of work is typically in the order of a few cents to a few US dollars.

In addition to micro-tasks, there are cases of crowdsourcing also of complex tasks. For instance, InnoCentive deals with problem solving and innovation projects, which may yield payments of thousands of US dollars (Howe 2008). Software development tasks are more akin to the latter as they are often interdependent, complex, heterogeneous, and can require extended periods of time, significant cognitive effort and diverse sets of expertise.

A number of potential benefits may arise through the use of crowdsourcing in general, and these would also be applicable in the context of software development:

- Cost reduction through lower development costs for developers in certain regions, and also through the avoidance of the extra cost overheads typically incurred in hiring developers;
- Faster time-to-market through accessing a critical mass of necessary technical talent who can achieve follow-the-sun development across time zones, as well as parallel development on decomposed tasks, and who are typically willing to work at weekends, for example;
- Higher quality through broad participation: the ability to get access to a broad and deep pool of development talent who self-select on the basis that they have the necessary expertise, and who then participate in contests where the highest quality 'winning' solution is chosen.
- Creativity and open innovation: there are many examples of "wisdom of crowds" creativity whereby the variety of expertise available ensures that more creative solutions can be explored, which often elude the fixed mindset that can exist within individual companies, a phenomenon which has been labelled "near-field re-purposing of knowledge." [3]

Since the first three benefits mentioned above (cost, time and quality) directly address the three central problematic areas of the so-called "software crisis"

---

[3] http://www.topcoder.com/whatiseoi/ (accessed 5 October 2012).

(Fitzgerald 2011), crowdsourcing has the potential to become a common approach to software development (Begel et al. 2012; Kazman and Chen 2009). The benefit of tapping into the creative capacity of a crowd is captured well in a quote attributed to Sun Microsystems co-founder Bill Joy, *"No matter who you are, most of the smartest people work for someone else"* (Lakhani and Panetta 2007). As Lakhani and Panetta (2007) point out, completing knowledge-intensive tasks will become increasingly challenging in traditional closed models of proprietary innovation, if most of the knowledge exists outside an organization.

Research on crowdsourcing tends to focus on one of three perspectives: the worker (supplier) perspective, the system (crowdsourcing platform, e.g., AMT) perspective, and the requester (customer) perspective (Stol and Fitzgerald 2014b). Studies of crowdsourcing software development, or what LaToza et al. (2013) referred to as 'Crowd Development,' are scarce. This is particularly the case for crowdsourcing software development from the customer perspective.

Similar to the confusion surrounding the term 'crowdsourcing' in general, there is some confusion about what constitutes crowdsourcing in a software development context. In particular, crowdsourcing may be positioned as closely related to other strategies such as outsourcing (Herbsleb and Mockus 2003) and opensourcing (Ågerfalk and Fitzgerald 2008). For instance, open source is often cited as the 'Genesis' of crowdsourcing (Howe 2008, p.8; Kazman and Chen 2009; LaToza et al. 2013), but others argue that open source is, in fact, not a form of crowdsourcing (Brabham 2013). Other terms that have been used as synonyms are 'peer production' (Feller et al. 2008) and 'commons-based peer production' (Benkler 2002; Kazman and Chen 2009), both referring to the idea that software is developed by a group of peers. While these strategies are similar in some respects, there are significant differences that set crowdsourcing apart (Surowiecki 2005).

1.4 Positioning the Sourcing Strategies

The three sourcing strategies that this book focuses on are alternatives to the 'traditional' outsourcing strategy. It is informative to position these alternative strategies with respect to conventional outsourcing. Figure 1.1 presents outsourcing and the three alternatives discussed in this book along two dimensions. The first dimension is that of the degree of 'knownness.' In both innersourcing and outsourcing, the workforce is 'known,' although the degree to which varies slightly. Clearly, in a traditional outsourcing scenario, a customer knows who they deal with as contracts have been put into place and the work to be done has been specified. In inner source, developers will be known by their corporate identifier (e.g. a developer's corporate email address). In opensourcing and crowdsourcing strategies, this is not the case. In these approaches, developers are generally unknown, although in an outsourcing approach, developers may make themselves known, or the opensourcing customer may still have their developers work on the opensourced project.

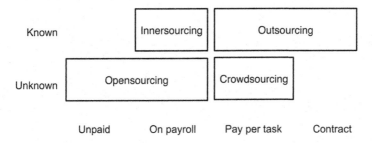

Fig. 1.1 Positioning of sourcing strategies

The second dimension in Fig. 1.1 represents the type of payments. Developers involved in an opensourcing context may or may not be paid. An opensourced project is, first of all, an open source project and may therefore attract volunteer developers, similar to 'conventional' open source projects. At the same time, the organization that opensourced the project in the first place, may still stay involved in the project and pay its developers to further maintain the project. Developers in an inner source project are, by definition, always paid as they are employees of an organization.

Developers in a 'conventional' outsourcing context may be paid either 'per task,' (short term) or they may be contracted (long term). Crowdsourcing, then, differs from outsourcing (besides that developers are unknown) in that developers are never 'contracted' in a crowdsourcing setting, but always paid per task.

1.5   Book Outline

The remainder of this book is structured as follows.

Chapter 2, based on a study by Ågerfalk and Fitzgerald (2008), discusses opensourcing with real world case studies at Iona Technologies, Philips and Telefonica.

Chapter 3, based on studies by Stol et al. (2014) and Stol and Fitzgerald (2015), discusses innersourcing with real world case studies at Philips Research and Philips Healthcare.

Chapter 4, based on a study by Stol and Fitzgerald (2014a), discusses crowdsourcing with a real world-case study based on the TopCoder crowdsourcing platform.

In Chaps. 2–4 we introduce a number of 'cues' as a way to capture critical components and lessons learned that signify important messages to managers and developers who are facing software sourcing decisions.

Finally, in Chap. 5 we conclude by presenting a comparison of the key findings from Chaps. 2–4. Based on this comparative analysis, a number of implications are outlined that readers should be aware of when considering how best to leverage "the unknown workforce."

Chapter 2
Opensourcing

In this chapter we discuss and illustrate opensourcing with case studies at IONA Technologies, Philips Healthcare and Telefonica. The chapter draws on the study reported by Ågerfalk and Fitzgerald (2008) and uses the set of company and community cues derived in that study (in the original publication, these were referred to as obligations). In the study, we asked both company and community interviewees to discuss their perceptions of their own obligations, and also the obligations they would expect from each other. It quickly emerged that many of these obligations were symmetrical. The study represents an important step towards both (a) elaborating the software sourcing research agenda to incorporate also this novel and unconventional approach to global sourcing and co-opetition, and (b) bringing the under-explored area of company-led open source projects onto the open source research agenda, in particular the liberation of hitherto proprietary software. As noted above, most research on outsourcing has adopted a single perspective: the customer or the supplier (but most often focusing on the customer), while this study considered both the customer (in this case, the company) and the community obligations. This is important since although the cues are symmetrical to a large extent, they are also complementary, and there are differing emphases from each perspective, both sides of which must be fulfilled to achieve a successful opensourcing arrangement. The study also identifies the significant ways in which opensourcing differs from conventional outsourcing—the lack of a formal contract and requirements specification driven by the customer as well as the absence of payment in the conventional sense, for example.

Seeking both theoretical and practical implications (Ågerfalk 2015), the study followed a mixed methods research design (Ågerfalk 2013; Venkatesh et al. 2013) in which qualitative interviews in three case companies were followed by a survey across several opensourcing projects. Further details on the research design can be found in an earlier publication on this study (Ågerfalk and Fitzgerald 2008).

The chapter continues as follows. Sect. 2.1 provides some background to the projects studied. Sects. 2.2 and 2.3 presents the company and community cues that

© The Author(s) 2015
P.J. Ågerfalk et al., *Software Sourcing in the Age of Open*, SpringerBriefs
in Computer Science, DOI 10.1007/978-3-319-17266-8_2

were identified and Sect. 2.4 elaborates on differences in perception of obligations between company and community. Finally, Sect. 2.5 summarizes the identified opensourcing cues and Sect. 2.6 elaborates on implications for practice.

2.1 Background to Case Study Projects

IONA Technologies—The Celtix Project: IONA Technologies, at the time of the study a NASDAQ-quoted company headquartered in Dublin, Ireland, with U.S. headquarters in Waltham, Massachusetts and offices worldwide. IONA was founded as a campus company at Trinity College Dublin in 1991, and provided products and services to help organizations build B2B enterprise portals. IONA was rated as the leading provider of standards-based platform middleware technology, with more than 4,500 blue-chip enterprise customers worldwide, who used IONA products to address large, complex application integration and achieve interoperability by means of a standards-based, service-oriented architecture. In June 2005, Iona extended its business model to incorporate open source by leading a community project to develop Celtix, an open source Java Enterprise Service Bus that was to co-exist with Artix, the company's flagship integration product. The Celtix project was hosted by an established open source community, ObjectWeb, who specialized in developing open source middleware products. Most of ObjectWeb's members were small to medium-sized enterprises based in continental Europe. The Celtix project achieved an impressive development productivity schedule, proceeding through four significant development milestones, a beta release to a fully stable 1.0 release in just over 10 months.

Philips Healthcare—The DVTk Project: Philips Healthcare (at the time of the study, Philips Medical Systems) specializes in medical devices and is part of the global technology organization Philips, headquartered in Eindhoven, The Netherlands. DICOM (Digital Imaging and Communication in Medicine), initiated in 1993, is a global standard for storing and processing medical images and is used in virtually all hospitals worldwide. The DVTk product provides extra functionality for problem solving and improving the quality of the DICOM interface. It begun as a collaboration between Philips and AGFA, and was released as open source under the GNU LGPL license in June 2005. Since then a community has grown up around the product with contributions from independent developers worldwide as well as developers in AGFA and Philips.

Telefonica—the Morfeo Project: Telefonica I+D, the R&D division of Spanish telecom operator Telefonica, initiated the Morfeo project which operated in the area of Service Oriented Architectures and aimed to speed up the development of software standards in this area. Telefonica I+D was the customer "engine," releasing proprietary software components and injecting resources into the community. The project set up its own Morfeo implementation of a SourceForge-like portal, where the development base of the sub-projects integrated in Morfeo were hosted, including source repositories, binaries, mailing lists, bug and changes trackers, and documentation.

2.2 Company Cues

2.2.1 *Do Not Seek to Dominate and Control Process*

Conventional software engineering and outsourcing wisdom suggest that explicit and comprehensive requirements specifications are critical to project success. Apparently this seems to be at odds with the open source development model which is predicated on the principle of a developer perceiving 'an itch worth scratching,' to use Raymond's (2001) memorable phrase. Also, open source developers have typically been users of the software being developed (Dinh-Trong and Bieman 2004; Gacek and Arief 2004; Mockus and Herbsleb 2002), and the software was often targeted to a horizontal domain (such as office desktop applications or software development tools). In such situations, clear requirements specifications are not necessary as the requirements are widely understood and internalized by the individual developers. Raymond's (2001) characterization of the cathedral v. the bazaar to differentiate open source development from traditional software development caused the perception that open source development was merely about developers following their own agenda developing in parallel in a spirit of optimistic concurrency. However, Raymond's characterization was based on a limited sample of open source projects which did not reflect the heterogeneity of the open source development landscape even at the time. In recent times, open source development has become more formalized. This is evident in the regular project meetings which are now a feature of a number of popular open source products, such as the Apache conferences in the US and Europe, the Zope/Plone and PyPy development sprints, and the GNOME annual project conferences (German 2005) which bring together developers to coordinate and plan development. As open source development is increasingly being purposely 'steered' as customers seek to stimulate open source development in specific vertical domains (such as automotive or telecoms) where a developer may not perceive an itch worth scratching. In these development situations, clear specifications could indeed be important. This increasingly explicit formalization of specifications is already evident in the commercially sponsored projects that are increasingly becoming a feature of the open source landscape.

Interviewees, however, stressed the manner in which requirements specification in opensourcing differed from traditional outsourcing. Companies may have a clear idea of what functionality they would like to see the community adding to the product. However, there has to be consensus as to what functionality will be added. If a company pushes its own agenda too much in seeking to control development, there can be problems. The Celtix project manager within IONA expressed it well:

> A company cannot just go onto the mailing list or the community, and say 'Can you guys build this?' When kicking off the project in the open source community, it's about stating the overall goal and the top-level requirements you are trying to achieve. Then it's driven by consensus. If people perceive you as driving your own agenda, then you will get pushback on having things accepted.

This again emphasizes the delicate equilibrium that must be maintained between acceptable open source community values and customer desire for value creation (Fitzgerald 2006). Interestingly, it was stressed that within the ecosystem formed around this mode of development, it was quite permissible for customers to engage in more traditional outsourcing relationship directly with some developers in the community, outside the strict remit of the opensourcing project.

Also, it was often the case that the initial development community contributions were to provide something that existed within their repertoire. Thus, their contributions were not based on an assessment of the most pressing commercial priority for the company; rather they considered what they could offer based on their existing repertoire and expertise.

2.2.2 Provide Professional Management and Business Expertise

The importance of strong management support has been verified in several studies of ICT adoption (e.g., Agarwal 2000; Chatterjee et al. 2002; Fichman 2004; Gallivan 2001). Project ownership and senior management championship is undoubtedly critical for radical, high-risk initiatives such as open source deployment since it contravenes the traditional model where ongoing support is legally guaranteed by a vendor. Indeed, top management championship is likely to become even more important in the future as open source adoption moves out of the domain of invisible infrastructure systems to more visible, high-profile desktop systems and applications.

Not surprisingly then, the company interviewees identified with a project ownership obligation. One customer interviewee stressed the radical change in mindset represented by opensourcing, suggesting that it represented a strategic initiative which differed from the normal business model where developers could see that their salary was pretty much directly derived from the sales of the commercial product that they developed. In the opensourcing model, their work could appear to be benefiting the open source community, and not leading to an obvious direct remuneration. Thus, top management championship was necessary to convince developers that the strategy made business sense. In fact, the Celtix project could also grow the market for other proprietary IONA products, enabling additional support contract revenue.

In keeping with demonstrating strong ownership and commitment to the project, IONA established a full time position—Open Source Program Director. This person is responsible for engaging with the community, and helps ensure that issues relevant to the open source community receive prompt attention which helps ensure the quality of the software. Also, senior management commitment can help ensure that R&D resources are provided. Interestingly, however, there is a delicate equilibrium to be maintained here also. The Celtix project manager at IONA suggested that if the project is seen as too much an IONA project, the developer community may have less interest in getting involved. A manager at Philips Healthcare summarized this dilemma:

> This application is deeply used within Philips organization. In several processes we depend on it. And because it's part of our product release, we want to stay in control of it. So on the one hand you want to control the project, and then on the other hand you want to be an open project and provide freedom for independent developers to join. And there's a little bit of conflict between these positions.

Several interviewees emphasized the need for the company to market the attractiveness of the project and improve its visibility. This has a twofold purpose. Firstly, the development community will perceive their reputation has been improved through involvement in a high-profile project with a high profile company. As a DVTk community interviewee expressed it: *"working with them [the company] is almost a sort of professional honor, as it were."*

This helps ensure the vibrancy of the project, and can attract further developers to the community, which cannot be taken for granted in a traditional open source project. Few open source projects to date have been deliberately started and nurtured to be successful; rather some extremely successful ones have emerged over time, whereas others have died off. Again, the Celtix project manager offered an interesting insight:

> There are a lot of open source projects which don't go anywhere, even though they have built good code. It also needs to be pushed so that it gets noticed and used by other projects, documented and marketed. This is a big overhead, and commercial companies have structures in place to help achieve that.

Interviewees also suggested that the customer company could provide their expertise in relation to software commercialization and productization in creating a professional open source product and subsequently marketing that product. This would involve a holistic approach and proactive marketing to ensure that all who could usefully consume the product were made aware of it, and could contribute. It was felt that a commercial vendor could usefully complement the open source community by providing this expertise. These efforts grow public awareness of the product, which can then create business-consulting opportunities for members of the development community. A DVTk community interviewee captured the essence of this well:

> What I am looking for is a multiplier. I am providing a piece of my work. I know they [the company] already have a useful chunk of work. But adding my bit to their larger existing work in a cooperative way creates something of greater multiplied use to everybody, including myself.

Given that there is a strong external element in opensourcing, customer interviewees stressed the necessity for clear project milestones and more visibility about product releases. This was contrasted with traditional proprietary development where internal milestones and actual release times are perhaps deliberately kept vague, whereas the need for the customer to be clear about future project plans was important to the community. More frequent product releases was identified as a by-product of the open source approach.

Also, it was suggested that the customer could not insist on a particular project-monitoring regime. Rather, different open source communities may have different norms and approaches in this area, and the customer has to be flexible and prepared to adapt to the particular regime in vogue in the particular open source community.

Related to transparency there was also a community expectation that the company have an open process for accepting community contributions. Interestingly, the company can have unrealistic expectations as to the level and significance of contributions. Indeed, one company manager suggested his experience was that of *"one significant contribution per month from the external community."*

Related to this is the issue of licensing and Intellectual Property (IP). A senior community interviewee with a background in commercial development suggested that it was sensible and pragmatic to have a clear IP policy. They had requested that IONA release the Celtix project under the Lesser General Public License (LGPL) and IONA agreed. The Celtix project manager suggested that IONA were keen to embrace open source and build trust within the community, and the choice of license is a key determinant for developers in deciding whether to participate in a particular open source project, and also for companies to adopt. Thus, the development community tends to have a preference for a restrictive (so-called viral or reciprocal) GPL-style license that safeguards their contributions due to its reciprocal nature. However, companies may tend towards more permissive licenses that afford them greater control over the future of the software. IONA had perceived the need to be even more open to other companies and communities, and hence dual licensed Celtix under the less restrictive Eclipse Public License also.

Related to this issue was the idea raised within Philips Healthcare of creating a single legal entity or foundation to represent the project. This trend towards legal incorporation has been established in several open source projects (O'Mahony 2005).

2.2.3   Help Establish an Open and Trusted Ecosystem

It was seen as important that both company and the community members strive towards the creation of a sustainable ecosystem around the product. A vital factor here is to create an atmosphere of trust. Creating an ecosystem and engendering trust is also facilitated by the fact that the project interaction tended to be "very much techie to techie" as one interviewee put it. The Celtix project management committee is chaired by an IONA Distinguished Engineer who would garner respect from the technical open source development community.

There was broad agreement from the community interviewees on this issue also. However, one community interviewee stressed the importance of meaningful content in the feedback. While promptness was appreciated, this evaporated if the content of the feedback was "empty." However, the "techie to techie" nature of the relationship helped ensure that feedback was meaningful.

Another issue with significant implications for project management practices within the customer company emerged in relation to development staff rotation. Normally, within proprietary software development companies, development staff are rotated after a few months onto other projects. However, because of the strong techie-to-techie interaction between developers in the company and community, there was a strong pressure from the community that developers would remain on the project for a lengthy period. This is in turn matched by the company expectation that community developers show strong loyalty and commitment to the project. The duration of involvement with the project is an aspect that varies across the different forms of outsourcing and is discussed in further detail in Chap. 5.

2.3   Community Cues

2.3.1   Clear and Democratic Authority Structure and Process Transparency

In the absence of traditional organizational sanctions, some form of structure is necessary to coordinate development. In many open source projects, this takes the form of 'benevolent dictatorship' as initially suggested by Raymond (2001). Several studies of open source development have detailed the complex authority structure that evolves over time to ensure that all code contributions are vetted and incorporated in a disciplined fashion (Mockus et al. 2002). Moreover, open source development has typically been characterized by the developers proactively taking charge, solving problems independently with minimal customer involvement, and without the need for traditional organizational sanctions to ensure development work is undertaken. Initially, open source developers did not engage in formal requirements analysis with customers (Scacchi 2002), but took direct responsibility for development decisions. Even though the open source development process is becoming more formalized (Fitzgerald 2006), open source developers are still more likely to retain a strong sense of independence.

Community representatives also identified clear and transparent authority structures as important—indeed, one stressed that these are *"not only important, but mandatory."* It was argued that since professional involvement in open source is increasing, the open source development community is expected to show the same level of quality and transparency as could be expected from any professional organization—people need to understand how decisions are made. Indeed, professionalism is permeating opensourcing projects since *"everybody knows there are business reasons why people are there,"* as pointed out by an IONA project manager, and also emphasized by a DVTk community member confessing that *"Getting good karma is great, but it's not my primary objective."* When the opensourcing community involves a large number of 'traditional professionals,' this is particularly emphasized.

The company interviewees also agreed that clear authority structures are important. However, in opensourcing, authority structures are framed by a strong belief in democratic principles:

> It would be good to ensure that that the [democratic] process is working, but I'm not sure that it is possible to see any authority structures other than that. It will always be shared responsibility.—Distinguished Engineer, IONA.

It was furthermore pointed out that such structures are important in two different respects. Firstly, they provide consistency between projects, which means that developers can easily contribute to more than one project. Contributing to several projects is not uncommon in OSS, and with the increasing interest in the so-called 'whole product approach' (Fitzgerald 2006), this is expected to be increasingly important—a point stressed by the Open Source Program Director at IONA. Secondly, they provide for consistent terminology within and across projects which ensures people are *"on the same page, and really focus on innovation."*

As a complement to clear authority structures, the lack of a traditional written outsourcing contract means that an open source community must be clear also about their actual work processes. Interestingly, this mirrors the transparency and close project monitoring that is expected on the part of the company.

2.3.2 Responsible and Innovative Attitude

OSS developers have long been acknowledged as being highly talented (Raymond 2001), and the loyalty of developers in the longevity of their commitment to their development projects has been remarkable (Feller and Fitzgerald 2002). Indeed, the cardinal sin of OSS, that of project forking (whereby a project is divided in two or more streams, each evolving the product in a different direction), is a strong community norm that acts against developer turnover on projects.

Although community and company interviewees alike believed it to be essential that the community takes responsibility and delivers on what has been committed to, this becomes somewhat blurred in the opensourcing context. In the Celtix project, for example, paid IONA employees do a large part of the overall development. Hence, the company has the power to manage part of the development effort more directly than would be possible in a traditional offshore outsourcing context. Although this may change as a project matures and the number of external contributions increases, an IONA project manager explained that there seemed to be a feeling that *"there will always be customer involvement."* However, he also suggested that a lot more community independence was expected in the future and that responsibility follows naturally with independence. A Manager at Philips Healthcare captured this crisply, referring to a potential problem with lack of written contracts:

> I think one of the biggest risks you have in open source development is when someone says—yes I'm going to do that, and he doesn't put any effort into it, nothing is done.

This also supports the company expectation of achieving consensus on the development roadmap, which assumes that the open source community is innovative and contributes constructively to this roadmap. As this will have a positive impact on the project, the community is expected to help achieve a positive impact among the company's customers.

2.3.3   Help Establish a Professional and Sustainable Ecosystem

The particular characteristics of open source position it as a good exemplar of the 'whole-product' concept of a market-driven business approach that seeks to deliver a complete solution to the customer in terms of products and services (Moore 1999). In this scenario, developers do the coding while others complete the business model by adding sales and marketing services—necessary activities but ones in which developers may not be interested. The open source 'whole-product' approach is also larger than a single company or software product or service. Indeed, the network benefits of open source arise as a result of the size of the overall community and ecosystem. Thus, an inter-organizational network of interested parties with complementary capabilities can form an ecosystem to offer a professional product and service in an agile, bazaar-friendly manner. Company service requests can be routed to the most appropriate expert partner in the network, perhaps even to the developer who wrote the actual code.

Thus, as mentioned above, both company and community members are expected to aim for a sustainable ecosystem. Consequently, community members are expected to be loyal and committed to continued involvement in the project, which, as mentioned above, is a marked feature of open source projects. This was confirmed by a Telefonica manager who explained that *"a benefit that open source brings is that people are more prepared to commit,"* which also transfers across to customer developers who *"even though they're working on the same technology now commit more personally."*

From a community perspective, it was suggested that the high-quality software associated with the open source model is an indication that the 'human capital management' is working. It was also perceived that the quality of the code is a way to attract more business, which is essential for the ecosystem to develop. As open source is moving away from networks of individuals to networks of companies, if a contributor earns a reputation for producing high-quality code, customers will keep coming back for more. It is also the case that customers sometimes use the open source model to identify the best suppliers, who are then approached directly and contracted in a 'traditional' outsourcing model.

Opensourcing customers expect the open source model to attract "high calibre people" who understand the project domain very well without requiring additional training. The Open Source Program Director of IONA even argued that it attracts a certain personality, with traits not necessarily those traditionally associated with a "top-notch programmer." In her view, people are attracted by the open source model because they want to "build something better," they want to "get involved," and they want to "be part of a community"—in summary, *these are the kind of people that I would want on my team, whether I was doing open source or not.*"

Interestingly, open source community members do not necessarily see themselves as suppliers commissioned by a customer in the traditional sense. In fact, the open source community as represented by ObjectWeb sees its members not as open source developers but as "ecosystem developers." There seems to be a definite trend towards more organized open source communities, such as that of ObjectWeb. Hence, facilitating effective inter-organizational teams is to a large extent an intrinsic property of the opensourcing model. As indicated above, this is due to the merging of customer and community into one ecosystem: *"I don't consider IONA as a customer. IONA is a member"* was how the ObjectWeb Chairman described the situation. Opensourcing is thus not just about building good working relationships between customer and supplier. It is about "ecosystem development." Hence, although there are business reasons for people to participate, there is a lot more collaboration than in traditional outsourcing:

> In a traditional market you don't call up your competitor and be like, oh, well tell me what your stuff does. But in open source you do.—Open Source Program Director, IONA.

In opensourcing, the software developed is typically not aimed for end-users but is more likely to be tools and infrastructure components. Consequently, the customer and community participants typically share the same level of technical expertise— *"it is mostly developer-to-developer communication."* Therefore, there is no need for formal training. Instead, knowledge transfer is happening continuously "from one research lab to another" within the ecosystem. This was emphasized by the ObjectWeb Chairman who asserted that *"I don't speak about education or anything like that, I speak about exchange between researchers."* The Open Source Program Director at IONA acknowledged this view referring to it as "cross pollination." According to a Project Manager at IONA, knowledge transfer was also facilitated by an early and proactive focus on documentation as part of the work towards achieving consensus on a development roadmap discussed above (a customer obligation).

2.4   Company Versus Community Differences

To validate the interview findings, we also performed a survey among active company and community participants (Ågerfalk and Fitzgerald 2008). In a questionnaire we asked both company and community respondents to rate the importance of fulfillment of each other's expectations. The analysis revealed a number of issues on which company and communities differed. Significantly, community respondents were less positive than company respondents in relation to how open the company was to outside contributions. This suggests that the community were not fully persuaded that companies were living up to the expectation to accepting contributions from the community. Typically, in open source projects, a meritocracy emerges over time as developers 'prove' themselves and are allowed to commit contributions. The discrepancy between the company and community here suggests that companies are cautious about accepting outside contributions into the code base, but presumably a meritocratic structure could emerge over time, which would see companies overcoming this reluctance.

However, the company respondents also differed from community respondents in that they were less positive about how the community provided a transparent authority structure to allow the company see the decision-making process within the community. This suggests that companies did not always perceive communities as being open in relation to development decisions, and also that the community might be remiss in relation to helping grow the public profile of the project. Given that companies see opensourcing as a means of growing product awareness, this is an obvious point of potential conflict, as companies would expect the community to help in this regard.

We also measured respondent opinion as to the success of opensourcing. However, there were no statistically significant differences between the company and community respondents. See Ågerfalk and Fitzgerald (2008) for details.

2.5 Summary of Opensourcing Cues

Altogether, the company and community cues identified above form a reciprocal set of cues that highlight important factors to consider when engaging in an opensourcing relationship. These are summarized in Table 2.1.

Table 2.1 Summary of company and community cues

Company Cues	Community Cues
Do not seek to dominate and control process	**Clear and democratic authority structure and process transparency**
• Not too forceful and dominant in pushing own agenda	• Provide a transparent authority structure to allow customer see the decision making process within the community
• Accept a general roadmap (vision) of future functionality rather than seeking a precise requirements specification	• Behave as a professional team
Provide professional management and business expertise	**Responsible and innovative attitude**
• Preserve continuity by keeping developers on projects for a longer period than the norm in proprietary software development	• Take responsibility and deliver on what is committed to
• Provide a business opportunity for the community to use the product	• Be creative and innovative in suggesting new functionality and directions for the project
• Provide professional expertise in relation to marketing and productizing the software	• Help achieve a positive impact among customers
• Provide R&D resources to further develop the project	
• Provide senior management commitment to the project	

(continued)

Table 2.1 (continued)

Company Cues	Community Cues
Help establish an open and trusted ecosystem	**Help establish a professional and sustainable ecosystem**
• Behave as a responsible member of the opensourcing ecosystem	• Offer high quality people who understand the project domain very well without requiring additional training
• Open to outside contributions	• Exhibit loyalty and continued involvement in the project
• Transparent in plans for the future of the project	
• Seek to create trust in the relationship with the community	
• Engage in community-sustaining activities	

2.6   Implications for Practice

Given that the opensourcing phenomenon has only recently emerged, success is not guaranteed. Our study findings can thus function as a checklist of salient issues for customers and communities engaging in opensourcing. The symmetrical and complementary nature of the company–community relationship illustrates how obligations and expectations need to be operationalized differently by the customer and community, but managed jointly, to ensure achievement of the mutual goal of a particular opensourcing initiative. Here we identify the potentially problematic issues that companies need to be aware of, and we also identify some new practices, or significant changes to traditional practices that are required.

2.6.1   Complementariness of Expectations: Product Lifecycle

While the company must be prepared to compromise at all stages and not seek to dominate and control the opensourcing process, the community must provide a transparent and democratic authority structure with shared responsibility. Furthermore, while the company must also be tactful and seek to embrace the open source values of openness and democracy, the community must be able to show the same level of management capability as would be expected from a traditional outsourcing partner. It is important that the company avoids pushing too hard its own agenda and accepts that requirements evolve throughout the project with active input from the community. To reciprocate, the community must make sure that its development process is communicated and accepted by the company. Furthermore, the company has to provide complementary expertise in relation to product commercialization and marketing. In turn, the community is expected to help improve public perception and awareness of the product.

When viewed holistically, a product lifecycle is evident. Firstly, the community is expected to take responsibility and deliver on what is committed to. In turn, the company can provide R&D resources to complement and further develop innovative ideas, and also provide its professional expertise in relation to marketing and productization of software, and in improving the visibility of the product. Furthermore, the credibility provided by the company in marketing a product can create a business opportunity for the product which community developers can then leverage.

Furthermore, the company must seek to reach consensus on the project monitoring system that will be instituted, on trying to show leadership and ownership of the project but not so strongly as to deter the development community. Overall, the company must achieve that delicate equilibrium between value-creation in terms of a successful business model for itself while not transgressing the open source community values. This includes embracing open source values of openness to be trustworthy in the eyes of the community. On the other hand, the community must adopt a professional attitude and approach in order to be taken seriously in the corporate world.

2.6.2   Changes to Standard Development Management Practices

We already referred to the need for management support on the company side to ensure buy-in to a risky initiative where it appears as if the 'crown jewels'—the company's software—is being given away for free. Standard operating practices that tend to apply in the customer company may need to change. For example, more clarity is required in relation to software release milestones so the community can plan their own business opportunities. Also, more frequent product releases are likely rather than artificially separating product release functionality on the basis of the revenue that can be generated which is often the case with proprietary software product releases. Furthermore, the policy in companies of rotating developers onto different projects after a period of several months may not be sustainable as company developers become associated with the project in the open source community. The community develops a trusted relationship with a company developer and do not wish to see that relationship disturbed through the company moving developers on to other projects.

2.6.3   Global Recruitment: From Unknown to Known

The study also revealed that outsourcing to the open source community provides a significant opportunity for companies to headhunt top developers, whereby community members become also employees of the customer—hence moving from outsourcing to a largely unknown open source workforce towards recruitment of talented developers from the open source community. In this study we see a move from 'unknown unknowns' as neither the customer nor the community are known to each other, to a scenario of 'known knowns' as each gets to understand each other's position and build complementary skills. Essentially, the opensourcing model consists of a company (as opensourcing customer) and a community of individual developers and other companies with whom the customer interacts. This community provides potential for development cost savings, recruitment opportunities, and the capability of increasing innovation. Interestingly, while the community is expected to behave professionally and provide transparent authority structures (thus reducing the 'unknown factor'), innovation potential is primarily to be expected from the 'unknown' part of the workforce. Hence, there are forces in the ecosystem pulling in opposite directions: while cost-savings and innovation are facilitated by a large 'unknown' workforce, trust-building and recruitment of community developers by the customer will tend to erode the unknown aspect.

This progression from unknown to known is also possible for innersourcing, and, but perhaps to a lesser extent, crowdsourcing. In the case of the latter, the competitive element and the fact that developers in the crowd tend not to build a relationship with a single customer (see Chap. 4) militates against this happening in a crowdsourcing context to some extent.

2.6.4 Open Source: From Replication to Innovation

Interestingly, open source is often assumed to be about replication rather than innovation. However, creativity and innovation is stimulated by multi-disciplinary teams operating outside conventional organization structures (Nonaka 1991; Garvin 1993; Leonard-Barton 1995; Inkpen 1996; Goldman and Gabriel 2005). Certain characteristics have been identified, including *autonomy* (which forms the basis for self-organizing and widens the possibility that individuals will motivate themselves to form new knowledge); *creative chaos* (whereby individuals do not have to follow organizational 'rules,' but are challenged to investigate alternatives and re-think assumptions); *information redundancy* (where individuals have information that goes beyond their immediate needs for a particular task); and *requisite variety* (whereby the individuals involved have the skill diversity to match the complexity and variety of the environment they face). Interestingly, these characteristics appear to be present in open source communities and can thus be expected to play an important part in the success of opensourcing as a software sourcing strategy. Studies of open source participation have suggested that about 40–50 % of open source developers are employed within professional organizations, suggesting an 'open' community of about 50–60 % (Lakhani and Wolf 2005; Jørgensen 2005; Riehle et al. 2014). This latter cohort may provide the creative and innovative spark as open source loses its image of being merely about imitation of proprietary products, and innovation becomes the defining feature. In this study, the characteristics of the community facilitate innovation as community developers operating outside traditional organizational constraints can identify new functionality and develop the software in creative ways—innovation does indeed seem to happen elsewhere (Goldman and Gabriel 2005).

2.6.5   Open Source: From Individual to Company

The study reveals an ongoing shift from open source as community of individual developers to open source as community of commercial organizations, primarily small and medium-sized enterprises, operating as a symbiotic ecosystem in a spirit of co-opetition. Overall the goal seems to be to create such a sustainable open and trusted ecosystem where customers and community participants operate as equals with neither party dominating. Thus, in contrast to traditional outsourcing, open-sourcing is not primarily about commissioning software development to a third-party, but rather about engaging in long-term collaborative activities leading towards a sustainable ecosystem. Since many of the collaborators in this ecosystem are likely to be the company's competitors, the collaboration is necessarily done in a spirit of co-opetition (Brandenburger and Nalebuff 1996). Both company and community members have a shared responsibility to actively contribute to the development and sustainability of the ecosystem. One way to ensure that this responsibility is honoured by the company is to do like IONA and appoint an Open Source Program Director. Other well known companies, including Google, HP and Microsoft, have done this as well.

Chapter 3
Innersourcing

The previous chapter discussed opensourcing, whereby the development and maintenance of a software product is "outsourced" to an open source community. As noted above, open source communities have developed a number of highly successful software products despite their seeming defiance of traditional software engineering wisdom. Starting in the late nineties, a number of organizations have begun to investigate how they could reproduce such success within their boundaries by adopting open source development practices for their in-house software development. This phenomenon has been termed 'Inner Source.' Most of these inner source cases started as grassroots initiatives, initiated by one or a few key individuals within these organizations. Since then, numerous organizations have embarked on inner source initiatives, including Ericsson, Samsung, and Sony Mobile. In this chapter we discuss and illustrate inner-sourcing with two case studies. This chapter draws on studies reported by Stol et al. (2014, 2015) and uses a set of nine cues (in the original publications, these were referred to as 'key factors') to consider in inner source initiatives. The studies presented in this chapter involved qualitative data gathered through a number of interviews with key participants of these initiatives. Further details on the methodology are reported by Stol et al. (2014). This chapter is organized as follows. Sect. 3.1 introduces the case studies. Sects. 3.2, 3.3 and 3.4 present the nine cues for inner source pertaining to the software product, practices and tools, and organization and community, respectively. Sect. 3.5 summarizes these nine cues. Sect. 3.6 concludes the chapter by discussing a number of implications for further research and practice.

3.1 Introduction to the Case Studies

The first case study of inner source presented in this chapter is an initiative at Philips Research. Earlier, two key members of this internal community had written a historical account of the project (Riemens and Van Zon 2006). The project, named

© The Author(s) 2015
P.J. Ågerfalk et al., *Software Sourcing in the Age of Open*, SpringerBriefs in Computer Science, DOI 10.1007/978-3-319-17266-8_3

Philips File Standard for Pictorial Data (PFSPD) was developed internally in the nineties for storing video sequences. At the time, Philips Research was conducting extensive research into video processing algorithms. Given the limited processing capacity of personal computers at the time, the company relied heavily on specialized and costly hardware. However, since other groups within the company also worked with video data, there was a need to implement the software on the PC platform, which was already widely available commodity hardware.

The second case is at a different division of Philips, Philips Healthcare, which is a large, globally distributed organization that develops and produces product lines of medical devices, such as X-ray and Magnetic Resonance Imaging (MRI) scanners. At the time of the study, the division had a workforce of almost 38,000. Philips Healthcare is organized in a number of "business units," each specialized and responsible for the development of their respective products.

3.2   Product Cues

We identified three cues that relate to the software product that is developed as an inner source project: seed product, multiple stakeholders, and modularity. Each of these is introduced with a brief synopsis followed by a more elaborate description and examples from the literature, and illustrated with two case studies.

3.2.1   Seed Product to Attract a Community

To 'bootstrap' an inner source initiative, there must be a 'seed' product—a shared asset—that is of significant value to the organization, or at least of high perceived value. The seed product is an initial and runnable version that can attract a community by first attracting users, who may subsequently become contributors (Wesselius 2008). This community of users and contributors is a key factor to an inner source project's success.

The need for an initial basic architecture and implementation was clearly noted by Raymond's (2001, p. 47) observation,

> It's fairly clear that one cannot code from the ground up in bazaar-style. One can test, debug and improve in bazaar-style, but it would be very hard to originate a project in bazaar mode. Linus didn't try it. I didn't either. Your nascent developer community needs to have something runnable and testable to play with.

Feller and Fitzgerald (2002) summarized this observation as follows: *"planning, analysis and design are largely conducted by the initial project founder, and are not part of the general OSS [open source software] development life cycle."* A real-world example of this is Topaz, which was an attempt to re-implement the Perl programming language. Its initiator, Chip Salzenberg, described this as follows,[1]

> when you're starting on something like this, there's really not a lot of room to fit more than one or two people. The core design decisions can't be done in a bazaar fashion.

Senyard and Michlmayr (2004) labeled this initial stage the 'Cathedral' phase, after which a project may transition into the 'Bazaar' phase. The Cathedral phase is characterized by an initial idea and implementation by an individual or small team; for instance, the inner source initiative at Alcatel-Lucent (an implementation of the Session Initiation Protocol (SIP)) started with a single developer (Gurbani et al. 2006). Once in its Bazaar phase as an inner source project, it attracted a significant community of users and developers within the organization which was pivotal for its further development. It has been suggested that the requirements and features of the seed product need not be fully known at the outset so that the project can benefit from organization-wide input and continuously evolve (Gurbani et al. 2006). If a project is fully specified and implemented (and thus only needs maintenance), there is little need for new contributions from a wider community. As Wesselius (2008) aptly pointed out, *"a bazaar with only one supplier isn't really a bazaar."* Dinkelacker et al. (2002) found that it is a challenge to find an appropriate initial software domain. Gurbani et al. (2006) hypothesized that lacking an initial seed product, *"a research or advanced technology group is a good location to start a shared asset,"* while Wesselius (2008) argued that the seed product should have a well-defined specification so that its development can be outsourced to a central development group (i.e., a core team). It is important that the shared asset has significant differentiating value to the organization; if it is merely a commodity (e.g., a database system or operating system), there may not be sufficient justification for in-house development (Van der Linden et al. 2009).

Philips Research is one such organization where an inner source initiative emerged (Stol and Fitzgerald 2015). The seed project was the implementation of a file format, Philips File Standard for Pictorial Data (PFSPD). This format had been developed internally for storing video sequences, a technology that was not as commonplace when it emerged in the nineties, at which time the processing capabilities of PCs were still limited and required special hardware. The file format was used for research on video processing algorithms that could subsequently be implemented in hardware. Over time, hundreds of different algorithms were implemented, all using the PFSPD format.

The seed product at Philips Healthcare was initially a set of components, or component suite, with common functionality related to the DICOM (Digital Imaging and Communications in Medicine) standard. This is a standard for exchanging medical images and workflow information, and as such, is used by most product groups within Philips. For that reason, this set of components was a good starting point, or *seed*, for Philips' inner source initiative. Over time, this component suite evolved into a platform for a software product line, which is still evolving and extended today.

---

[1] http://www.perl.org/pub/1999/09/topaz.html

3.2.2 Multiple Stakeholders for Variety in Contributions

An inner source project must be needed by several stakeholders (i.e., individuals, teams, or projects that productize the shared asset) so that members from across an organization can contribute their expertise, code and resources. This in turn will help to establish a sufficiently large pool of users and contributors to establish a vibrant inner source project.

Gurbani et al. (2006) argued that different product groups have different needs, and that groups can benefit from other groups' contributions. For instance, the SIP implementation at Alcatel-Lucent benefited greatly from feedback and suggestions of colleagues who were experts in specific fields, such as network optimization and parsing techniques. In other words, input from across an organization can significantly broaden the expertise that is available to a project (Riehle et al. 2009). Organization-wide feedback can help to solicit a variety of ideas, a sentiment that we would express (inspired by Linus's Law) as: *"Given enough mindsets, all ideas are obvious."*

The presence of multiple stakeholders suggests that there is considerable interest in the development of a software product; hence, this indicates a good motivation to pool resources and to develop it as an inner source project (Gurbani et al. 2006). Furthermore, having different product groups integrate the shared asset helps to manage its scope and reusability in different contexts (Robbins 2005). Robbins (2005) outlined the tension with conventional software development, in which teams try to optimize returns on their current project on the one hand, and the cost of providing ongoing support for reusable components on the other hand. From a business perspective, Gurbani et al. (2006) argued,

> It is essential to recognize and accommodate the tension between cultivating a general, common resource on the one hand, and the pressure to get specific releases of specific products out on time.

At Philips Research, the initial version of PFSPD was written by a few developers who identified a need to collaborate with teams based in the US. These teams did not have the specialized hardware infrastructure. A new version of PFSPD for (at that time) newer platforms running Linux therefore became a necessity to collaborate closely with other teams for research and implementation of video algorithms.

Philips Healthcare is a large organization with many product groups that use the inner source project as a platform. It is used in more than 300 products delivered by more than ten product groups. Such a large number of stakeholders offers opportunities for large-scale reuse, which is why software that offers common functionality is an appropriate choice for a shared asset.

3.2.3 Modularity to Attract Contributors and Users

An inner source project should have a modular architecture. This will facilitate parallel development as different developers (i.e., contributors) can work in parallel on different parts of the project without any merge conflicts. Furthermore, a modular architecture will also help reuse as integration can become easier, thus increasing the number of potential users.

A modular software structure has many advantages and is generally preferred (Parnas 1972) but is particularly important in open source style development, as it facilitates parallel development, that is, allowing many developers work on different parts of the same product simultaneously (Torvalds 1999; Bonaccorsi and Rossi 2003). Successful open source projects tend to exhibit a high level of modularity (O'Reilly 1999; Feller and Fitzgerald 2002). A modular architecture greatly helps in merging various changes into a single development branch (Gurbani et al. 2006) or even to let developers work on the same repository at the same time (with no merges needed). MacCormack et al. (2006) refer to this as "architecture for participation," the idea that modularity facilitates developers to better understand the code, and which thus enables developers to contribute in a meaningful way. Baldwin and Clark (2006) showed that codebases exhibiting a higher modularity help to increase developers' incentives to join and remain involved in an open source project, thus helping to keep contributors involved.

Another benefit of modularity is that it supports reuse of a component, which means that it helps to attract (and keep) users in the community. Reuse is a key motivation to start an inner source project in the first place (Dinkelacker et al. 2002; Vitharana et al. 2010). An inner source project will only attract users if it offers a significant set of functionality. However, when the shared asset becomes too "heavyweight," it may be perceived as too difficult or inconvenient to use. Dinkelacker et al. (2002) expressed this sentiment as follows: *"Using the word 'module' somewhat generically, it's a challenge to strike the balance between module simplicity and utility."* This trade-off refers to a component's completeness (utility) thereby broadening a product's appeal (Robbins 2005), and preventing feature creep, making reuse of the component undesirable due to its complexity or size. One of the principles of collaboration in open source is egalitarianism (Riehle et al. 2009), the idea that anyone is welcome to contribute a new feature to "scratch an itch" (Raymond 2001; Robbins 2005). However, this may also *"lead to feature creep and a loss of conceptual integrity"* (Robbins 2005). Losing 'conceptual integrity' may result in a component which is no longer easy to use or whose architecture imposes too many restrictions on the client-application.

PFSPD benefited from a well-designed API early on in the project. Additional utility tools (39 in total) were developed around the main library, such as converters, comparison tools and viewers. Given that these were developed as separate tools, the tool chain exhibited a great degree of modularity. At some point, maintaining and releasing these different tools was found to be a burden, and it was decided to integrate them into a single command-line application, while maintaining the original modular architecture.

Philips Healthcare's shared asset is a large (several millions of lines of code) and still growing piece of software. The platform initially started out as a 'component suite,' and this model was quite successful. However, the combination of different uses of the components yielded suboptimal results, in that the need for integration testing was not eliminated. For that reason, the core team moved to delivering 'component assemblies,' which are pre-integrated and tested half-products that product groups can use. While the components may be modular, they are not suitable for an a la carte approach, whereby only those components deemed useful are selected, as one participant described.

> The components are not so rich that you can choose component A, B, C and D. What you would do is configure the platform and within that configuration you'd choose A, B, C or D. It's more an integrated approach.

3.3   Practices and Tools Cues

The next set of cues relate to the development practices and tools to support that are used in an inner source project. These are: practices for development, practices for quality assurance, and development tools.

3.3.1   Practices to Support Bazaar-Style Development

Software development in an internal bazaar is inherently different from conventional approaches, including contemporary agile ones. Two aspects related to implementation activities are particularly different in open source development: requirements elicitation and maintenance. For an inner source project to succeed, developers should be comfortable with bazaar-style practices, as conventional approaches may not be appropriate.

In terms of requirements elicitation, the process of identifying a feature and providing an implementation is very different from traditional "requirements engineering" scenarios, and thus this is something that inner source developers should be comfortable with. Whereas conventional development approaches may have procedures in place that prescribe how requirements are gathered, stored, and managed, the requirements process in open source projects may have a much faster turnaround time from initial idea to implementation. Deliberation about features, details, and idealized systems is typically not much appreciated. This is not to say that open source developers do not discuss requirements at all, but that a sound balance must be found. On the one hand, conversations (e.g., on mailing lists or IRC) may lead to discussions (disputes, even) on the most minute and trivial details, a phenomenon known as "bikeshedding" (Fogel 2005, p.98). On the other hand, some community members may have the most fantastic plans and idea, but it is actual running code that is valued most. Linus Torvalds, benevolent dictator of the Linux kernel project, expressed this sentiment famously as *"Talk is cheap. Show me the code."* (Torvalds 2000). Thus, a common scenario is that developers identify features, provide a "patch" that implements the new functionality after which it is offered to the community for peer review. The fact that the feature was needed in the first place is *"asserted after the fact"* (Scacchi 2004).

As an open source project evolves, it is subject to maintenance. Open source projects slowly evolve, with many minor improvements and mutations, over many releases with short intervals. Or, as Merilinna and Matinlassi (2006) phrased it, *"OSS is a moving target—or a dead corpse."* A project founder may not have anticipated the project's evolution where the many additions of various features uncover the limitations of the initial design made in the project's Cathedral phase. As a result, contributors feel the need to re-implement a subsystem, or what Scacchi (2004) has termed "reinvention." Raymond cited Brooks (1995, p. 116), who captured this idea well: *"Plan to throw one away; you will, anyhow."* The Perl programming language is a good example of this. Perl versions one to four were incremental. Perl's creator, Larry Wall, reimplemented Perl 5 from scratch. However, at some point that code base was characterized[2] as *"an interconnected mass of livers and pancreas and lungs and little sharp pointy things and the occasional exploding kidney."* Around the year 2000, it was decided to re-implement the language once again, resulting in a thorough reinvention.[3] Reinvention in inner source may be more restricted than open source communities due to the pressure of productization and limited resources. In practice, therefore, reinvention is limited only to those parts of a product that are critical bottlenecks. For instance, the parser in the initial SIP implementation at Alcatel-Lucent was optimized for scalability by having an expert on parsing techniques from within the organization 'reinvent' it.

Within Philips Research, PFSPD was never an 'official' project but rather an initiative by motivated developers to tend to their needs. Since development was extra-curricular, work on PFSPD should be characterized as a series of development 'bursts'; whenever a new feature of improvement was necessary, and time was available, developers would work intensively on the project. Before a developer would work on a feature, this intention was usually announced on the mailing list, which sometimes resulted in feedback on the proposed approach.

Philips Healthcare, offering advanced systems for the medical domain, is operating in a regulated environment and as such its development process is subject to audits by regulators, such as the US FDA. Philips have extensive processes for how requirements move from product groups to the core team. Formal channels for communicating requirements include issue trackers and databases with "all sorts of procedures," but there are also a number of informal channels. These include mailing lists on which developers can provide support to people in other product groups.

Though an open source way of working suggests a central repository through which developers can improve the code and make changes as they see fit, this is not the case in Philips. While the source code of the common platform is accessible to all business units (facilitating developers in inspecting and understanding how features are implemented), individuals do not typically make changes directly, as one participant explained, *"It's not like every developer can check out a piece of the platform, change it, and check it back in."* Instead, a key concept in Philips' inner source initiative is that of co-development projects, whereby one or more members of the core

---

[2] http://www.perl.com/pub/1999/09/topaz.html

[3] http://www.perl6.org/archive

team work closely with a product group to develop (or enrich existing) functionality. Such 'co-development' of features ensures that the new software (a) adheres to the architecture of the shared asset, and (b) implements the new functionality correctly as required by the product group. A core team member that works closely with a product groups is what Gurbani et al. (2010) termed a "feature advocate."

3.3.2 Practices to Support Bazaar-Style Quality Assurance

One of the key tenets of successful open source projects is a set of mature quality assurance (QA) practices. For an inner source project to flourish and achieve a high level of quality, it is important that a set of QA practices are adopted that are suitable for an inner source project.

Open source quality assurance practices can differ significantly from those used in conventional software development. Peer review, which was briefly mentioned, is one of the best known practices in open source development (McConnell 1999; Rigby et al. 2012). Feller and Fitzgerald (2002, p. 84) characterized peer review in open source settings as truly independent; that is, peer-review in open source projects is a self-selected task by other interested developers (Asundi and Jayvant 2007; Rigby et al. 2008). Open-source developers are more likely to provide genuine feedback given their interest in the success of the project they work on, rather than doing a review because they were told to and possibly having to consider relationships with co-workers when pointing out any issues with their contributions.

Peer review becomes particularly effective when there is a large number of developers in a project, as it can benefit from what is known as Linus's Law (Raymond 2001): *"Given a large enough beta-tester and co-developer base, almost every problem will be characterized quickly and the fix obvious to someone,"* more often stated succinctly as *"Given enough eyeballs, all bugs are shallow."*

Peer review can take place either before or after committing changes to the source code, depending on whether the contributor making the changes has a 'commit bit,' that is, write access. It is an important and effective practice to ensure that any code that is checked in is of good quality, does not contain hacks, and will not lead to an undesirable path of evolution (i.e., prevent future improvements). Direct commit access is usually only given to long-time developers who are trusted to protect the project from bad check-ins; such developers are also known as "trusted lieutenants" (Raymond 2001; Gurbani et al. 2006).

A cardinal sin is to "break the build," that is, checking in code that would prevent the project compiling successfully, as it puts all developers' progress on hold. In order to prevent this from happening, contributors are expected to test their changes first before submitting a patch. Regression test suites and use of specialized testing tools (e.g., Tinderbox) are commonly used in successful open source projects to provide monitoring of the quality.

Another practice to support quality assurance is to make regular and frequent releases (Robbins 2005; Michlmayr and Fitzgerald 2012; Michlmayr et al. 2015). Releases can be of different types, such as development releases or production releases that are more thoroughly prepared (or 'hardened') for productization. Release management in conventional software development can vary substantially, depending on the development approach that is taken (e.g., waterfall (Royce 1987) versus agile approaches such as Scrum). Likewise, while release management in open source projects can vary significantly as well (Erenkrantz 2003), successful open source projects tend to follow Raymond's advice: *"Release early. Release often. And listen to your customers"* (Raymond 2001, p. 29). In recent years, a number of successful open source projects have adopted a time-based release strategy, as opposed to a feature-based release strategy (Michlmayr and Fitzgerald 2012). Time-based releases offer various benefits, such as less "rushing in" code for new features as releases are frequent, and less fire-fighting as the release process is exercised more often. A regular release cycle also means that there are more opportunities for "bug squashing" sessions (usually held prior to a release), and more regular feedback of users, both of which can contribute to a project's quality. This practice is also very suitable for inner source projects; for instance, the SIP stack at Alcatel-Lucent used to be on a two-weekly (development) release schedule.

A key element of ensuring quality in the PFSPD project was that any problem reports from users would immediately be investigated. This way, issues were quickly resolved, which also built users' confidence in the quality of the project.

The operations subdivision of the core team in Philips Healthcare has responsibility for the verification and testing of the platform they deliver. Given the regulated domain, documentation on design and tests have to be delivered. This team runs system tests (as black box) and unit tests of individual components (as white box tests). The operations team also supports product groups in writing effective tests. In terms of frequent releases, the core team makes a new release approximately twice a year. These are stable and versioned releases, which are fully tested, documented, and supported. Since such releases represent new 'versions' of the platform accompanied with required test and design documentation, the core team must ensure there are no open issues, which makes such releases more costly and thus not very frequent.

Product groups also have the option to use a more recent snapshot that provides more 'cutting-edge' functionality, much like development releases found in open source development (Michlmayr and Fitzgerald 2012; Michlmayr et al. 2015). These facilitate early feedback to the core team, so that any issues can be resolved early. One product group leader described this as follows:

> We sit very closely with the platform team, with as many integrations as possible, and keep that feedback loop as short as possible, close to the OSS model, and that works much better. Much less hassle and trouble.

3.3.3 Standardization of Tools for Facilitating Collaboration

A key success factor for an inner source project is that there is a set of common and compliant development tools so as to make contributing easy (Dinkelacker et al. 2002; Gurbani et al. 2006; Riehle et al. 2009). Differences in the tools that are used across an organization (not uncommon in large organizations) can be an obstacle for developers to contribute, or may necessitate duplication of the code repository, causing additional synchronization efforts. For that reason, a set of common tools must be available throughout the organization.

Tools commonly used by open source projects are (besides compilers) version control systems (e.g., Subversion), issue tracking software (e.g., Trac), mailing lists, and wikis (Robbins 2005). While a number of these tools are also commonly used in commercial software development, different business units within large organizations often use a wide range of different tools (Robbins 2005; Gurbani et al. 2006; Riehle et al. 2009). Riehle et al. (2009) reported that *"The biggest hurdle to widespread adoption of SAP Forge is its limited compliance with tools mandatory for SAP's general software development process."* Several authors reported that moving code among different version control systems is challenging (Dinkelacker et al. 2002; Gurbani et al. 2006). For instance, Gurbani et al. (2006) reported their experiences of certain teams replicating the original shared asset's source code into their preferred repository, causing significant merging problems later on.

Therefore, an organization considering adopting inner source should pay sufficient attention to addressing this issue. Often, barriers to achieve this are not of a technical nature, but rather organizational or sometimes political. Organizational policies enforced by IT departments of large, global organizations may have significant impact on what can be achieved, even if supported by local management.

The PFSPD project benefited greatly from the common set of tools that were used early on in the project. This proved particularly useful when one of the core team members moved to a different division based in the USA. Having the necessary infrastructure already available for distributed development, development continued seamlessly after this move, and with the newly introduced time difference, development could 'follow the Sun' during bursts of development.

Philips Healthcare use a toolset that is provided using a Software-as-a-Service (SaaS) model by an external supplier. The core team has an "Operations" subdivision that provides operational support for the development environment that is rolled out throughout the organization. This ensures that all product groups have the same development environment, which prevents the various problems associated with different toolsets.

3.4 Organization and Community Cues

The last set of cues relate to the environment within which development takes place, namely an organization as well as the developers within that environment: the community. These three cues are: coordination and leadership, transparency, and company support and motivation.

3.4.1 Coordination and Leadership to Support Meritocracy

An inner source project requires a bazaar-style approach to coordination and leadership so as to allow a core team, trusted lieutenants, and other motivated contributors to emerge. Providing flexibility to members across an organization is key to enabling a community to flourish.

Leadership and coordination are two aspects that differentiate open source projects from traditional projects. Several authors have highlighted the importance of leadership, including a core team that takes responsibility for development and maintenance of a shared asset (Dinkelacker et al. 2002; Gurbani et al. 2006, 2010; Wesselius 2008). Leadership in traditional organizations is based on seniority and status (e.g., junior v. senior developer) (Riehle et al. 2009). This is very different from open source communities, where projects are typically started by one developer who acts as a benevolent dictator, such as Larry Wall (Perl), Guido van Rossum (Python) and Linus Torvalds (Linux kernel).

As a project matures, new key developers can emerge based on the concept of meritocracy (Gacek and Arief 2004; Neus and Scherf 2005; Riehle et al. 2009). Status is earned based on the merit of a developer's contributions, which usually also results in a bigger say in important decisions regarding the project. Gurbani et al. (2006) reported the following:

> Some developers will naturally gravitate towards understanding sizeable portions of the code and contributing in a similar manner, often on their own time. Such developers should be recognized by making them the owner of particular subsystems or complex areas of the code (the "trusted lieutenant" phenomenon).

Whereas in traditional organizations coordination is based on project plans and release schedules, open source projects are rather self-organizing (Crowston et al. 2007). Open source developers, not concerned with schedules or deadlines, typically select tasks that they are interested in (Feller and Fitzgerald 2002; Robbins 2005; Riehle et al. 2009). The motivation to do so is often explained as *"scratching an itch"* (Raymond 2001). Torkar et al. (2011) identified task selection as an opportunity for commercial software development organizations to adopt a bazaar-style of working; letting go of formal structures and ownership was also suggested by Dinkelacker et al. (2002). However, inner source projects cannot be fully self-organizing, as there are business aspects to consider such as the timely delivery of products that depend on the shared asset. Thus, self-organization is one area where the open source approach needs to be tailored, or renegotiated to fit a corporate context. In the case of Alcatel-Lucent, for example, Gurbani et al. (2010) identified a number of project management roles within their core team. A key role is that of the feature manager, that is, someone who performs a certain level of coordination. For instance, the feature manager identifies features that need to be implemented and will identify potential developers in the wider organization who would be suitable work on a particular feature. This process depends partly on knowledge of who-knows-what and involves finding a balance between developers' availability and engaging in a dialogue with those developers' managers so as to be able to "borrow" them.

The core team and trusted lieutenants previously mentioned must agree on a common vision for future evolution of the project (Gurbani et al. 2006) and guard the common architecture so that additions from one contributing group do not lead to integration problems in another group.

The PFSPD 'core team' consisted of four key members, but other developers contributed as well. The developer community of the project was very limited in size, with a slightly bigger community of several tens of users.

In Philips Healthcare, a Steering Committee decides on the new features that will be delivered in the next version, which provides a high-level form of coordination. Sometimes, the core team gives priority to certain business units for a certain release when planning the implementation of new features. Some groups are not eager to contribute but are more passively waiting for the platform team to implement new functionality. By more actively contributing, a product group gets more control over new features and functionality, which helps ensure that the new code does what the product group needs. One participant remarked that the groups involved from the beginning have been most successful in getting their requirements implemented.

3.4.2   *Transparency to Open Up the Organization*

Transparency lies at the heart of, and is a prerequisite for, open collaboration projects, even when this 'openness' is limited to an organization's boundaries, as is the case for inner source. Transparency is essential to establish visibility and to attract interested developers who may start out as 'lurkers' and transform into active contributors. We discuss three aspects of transparency: organizational culture, artifacts and communication.

Neus and Scherf (2005) suggested learning about the organization's culture and whether there is a strictly obeyed hierarchy. They suggest to do the "Emperor's clothes" test in order to see how open the organization is, describing this as follows:

> We find out if there are ways in the organization that allow a novice (e.g., an intern) to publicly call attention to the emperor's (i.e., the expert's) lack of clothes (i.e., to raise quality issues), or if all internal communication addressed to a larger audience has to go through some gatekeepers.

An open development culture was also advocated by Riehle et al. (2009), who argued in favor of egalitarianism, and that *"projects must exhibit a mind-set that welcomes whoever comes along to help, rather than viewing volunteers as a foreign element."* Raymond (2001), too, argued that it is critical that a coordinator is able to recognize good design ideas from others. Dinkelacker et al. (2002) reported that "getting developers and their management chain comfortable with sharing code and development responsibility across the company" may be challenging.

Open collaboration projects provide universal, immediate access to all project artifacts, allowing anyone to participate (Robbins 2005; Riehle et al. 2009). While a set of common tools facilitates the more technical aspects that ensure a common development environment, infrastructure is essential for a transparent process that is based on sharing information and keeping information widely available and up-to-date. The extent to which project artifacts (source code, issues, documentation, etc.) are accessible to others in commercial software development settings varies widely from organization to organization. It is not uncommon that such artifacts are private to the development team.

It is important also that access is straightforward and that there are no barriers to finding information on an inner source project, so that potential new community members do not find getting involved to be too cumbersome. At Alcatel-Lucent, for instance, a Centre of Excellence (COE) was established, that provided infrastructure for accessing the source code as well as other information on the inner source project (Gurbani et al. 2006). This way, the COE established a "one-stop shop" for users of the shared asset. It is important to provide sufficient support and maintenance for this and other infrastructure that is needed for inner source (Dinkelacker et al. 2002).

Other infrastructure includes means of communication, such as a mailing list for online (and archived) discussions, IRC for synchronous and real-time communication, and Q&A forums. More mature open source projects can also organize regular meetings in an IRC channel. For instance, the Parrot project[4] has weekly progress meetings to which all developers with a "commit bit" are invited. This is very different from conventional communication mechanisms, such as scheduled meetings, where face-to-face communication is much more common than in open source projects (where face-to-face communication is minimal if not non-existent). Agile methods in particular value face-to-face meetings over written reports and memos. Though organizations involved in distributed development lack face-to-face communication as well, modern technological infrastructure (e.g., video conferencing) facilitates virtual face-to-face meetings, which are highly uncommon in open source projects. In any case, meetings in commercial organizations are less "bazaar-like" in that participants are not supposed to join or leave as they please.

Transparency also played a role in the PFSPD project. Initially, access to the source code repository was limited to the core developers, but it became an inner source project once the source code was migrated to an internal SourceForge installation. Two separate mailing lists provided the main channels for communication: a developer list to discuss daily development and progress, and a user list to support the user community. New releases were downloaded several tens of times.

Philips Healthcare uses tools and infrastructure provided by CollabNet to support an (internal) online community and facilitate a transparent process. This includes a mailing list on which people can post questions and comments. Developers and architects follow these lists and respond to issues that they are familiar with. This

---

[4] www.parrot.org

does not mean that all communication is online; architects still have face-to-face meetings to discuss architectural roadmaps. Chief architects also provide training sessions targeting product groups. However, the day-to-day knowledge sharing regarding issues and usage of the shared asset is greatly improved by the online communication as one participant explained.

> Our Inner Source initiative really helps [for knowledge sharing] because we see that the communication between developers is much more interactive. Since we've changed from a central team that delivers a binary platform to the new Inner Source model in which everybody could see the source code and also contribute, we saw the community growing. People started to inform each other about dos and don'ts about the design. And people found out much quicker whether others were using the platform correctly. That community became much more lively when we adopted the Inner Source model.

3.4.3 Management Support and Motivation to Get People Involved

A key condition for establishing a successful inner source project is to acquire top-level management support on the one hand and to involve interested people (i.e., users and contributors) in an organization on the other hand. Support from top-level management is required so that additional resources can be granted if requested, and also for advertising and advocating an inner source project throughout the organization.

Several authors have argued for the importance of management support (Dinkelacker et al. 2002; Gurbani et al. 2006, 2010; Riehle et al. 2009). Dinkelacker et al. (2002) described how this was a crucial factor for one of HP's inner source initiatives, which is named CDP.

> It has been critical to CDP success to have a group of executive champions. In CDP's case we have two champions, the chief technology officer and the chief information officer. These champions provide the urgency to the organization to start the change process.

Riehle et al. (2009) wrote that managers of research projects are generally supportive of the volunteer contributions, but that managers of volunteers from regular product groups are typically skeptical in the beginning. However, Riehle et al. also found that management became "neutral" or even supportive once they realized the benefits of early engagement with research projects. An important issue here is that this management support is also expressed in terms of budgets, that is, that budgets and resources are made available to support this. Wesselius (2008) discussed a number of criteria for an internal business model that can support this.

While management support is essential, merely enforcing an inner source initiative from the senior management level is not sufficient and in fact goes against the open source development philosophy that is characterized by voluntary participation (Wesselius 2008). Neus and Scherf (2005) emphasized the importance of passionate people: *"to drive change, you need passion,"* and *"people who understand and are excited about the change."* In a similar vein, Raymond (2001) wrote the following:

> In order to build a development community, you need to attract people, interest them in what you're doing, and keep them happy about the amount of work they're doing.

Neus and Scherf (2005) argued that the cultural shift needed for adopting a bazaar-style development approach cannot be forced but merely facilitated. In order to achieve motivation and "buy-in" of staff, it is essential to demonstrate value first, and suggest to do so by solving a concrete problem with a small scope. In order to get started, a few authors have suggested to provide what has been termed a "gentle slope" (Halloran and Scherlis 2002) to provide some handholding (Gurbani et al. 2010) or to define an "entry path" for newcomers (Torkar et al. 2011), which may eventually lead to an active community of contributors.

The PFSPD project was, as briefly mentioned, never an officially funded project assigned to a specific team. The collaboration between contributors emerged from their need to work on the software as that helped them in collaborating. However, due to the novelty of this collaboration model, for some contributors it was hard to justify their time spent on the project as management did not fully understand or appreciate their efforts, or the nature of the inner source initiative. For others, time spent on this project could be justified as a 'technology transfer' activity. The general appreciation from the project's users further kindled developers' motivation to sustain work on the project.

Management of Philips Healthcare strongly supports the inner source initiative. In the late nineties, management had started initiatives to improve reuse, which resulted in a software product line organization (Van der Linden et al. 2007). The organization has since acquired many companies, which have become product groups, all of which were encouraged to use the common platform. The inner source initiative helped to address a number of issues related to knowledge sharing, improving productivity. Furthermore, given the one-to-many relationship between the platform team and the product groups, the former could prove to be a bottleneck for the latter, an issue that could be alleviated by introducing Open Source-development principles. However, while management support is imperative, there is no central authority that prescribes to a product group what it should do, as a director of the technology office explained.

> We don't have the right to tell them, 'tomorrow you'll do this.' That's not how it works; it's more like building a case, discussing what would be wise.

Therefore, in order for any inner source initiative to succeed, product groups had to buy in. One co-development coordinator explained this as follows:

> The driver to do this [collaboration] is to ensure that what's implemented works for us. It's not to help others with that new functionality, it's primarily for us. But, once it's finished, then you'd also discuss this beforehand with the core team that the component can go back into the platform.

3.5 Summary of Cues for Inner Source

The nine cues for inner source are presented in Table 3.1, and are organized per category. The first three cues pertain to the software product that is being developed as an inner source project. The second set of three cues pertain to the practices and tools that are used to develop that product, and the third set of cues pertain to the organization and community within which the inner source project is established.

Table 3.1 Summary of innersourcing cues

Software Product cues	Practices and Tools cues	Organization and Community cues
Seed product to attract a community	**Practices to support bazaar-style development**	**Coordination and leadership to support meritocracy**
An initial product that developers can "play" with and run must be available to attract contributors	A waterfall approach does not work for inner source development. Instead a more flexible approach will allow developers to more quickly add features and fix defects	Those contributors who are most closely involved must be recognized as experts and trusted with important design decisions. Assigning tasks to developers is not appropriate; rather contributors must be left free to contribute as they see fit while negotiating with project leadership how this could be done best
Multiple stakeholders for variety in contributions	**Practices to support bazaar-style quality assurance**	**Transparency to open up the organization**
Drawing on expertise from a variety of people with different skills supports the 'requisite variety' characteristic that stimulates innovation	Rather than depending on a separate testing team or QA department, bazaar-style QA can benefit from large-scale peer-review and parallel debugging	Transparency means making available all artifacts such as source code and documentation and making the development process visible; e.g. discussions on archived mailing lists, IRC channels, etc.
Modularity to attract contributors and users	**Standardization of tools for facilitating collaboration**	**Management support and motivation to involve people**
A modular architecture is an "architecture for participation," which allows contributors to contribute in a meaningful way	A common set of tools is needed to let developers collaborate seamlessly on the same code base without version control issues	Management support is essential for inner source initiatives to flourish. On the other hand, inner source projects rely on the active involvement of motivated contributors and thus they should be encouraged to participate

3.6 Implications for Research and Practice

The idea of inner source was first mentioned around the late nineties, soon after open source attracted more attention from researchers and the software industry, who observed some significantly successful products coming from the open source domain. Some of the "early adopters" were companies such as Hewlett-Packard and Lucent. However, very little research has been conducted on the topic in the years since. This is surprising, given that there is considerable interest from industry on the topic in recent years. Many multinational companies have started inner source initiatives, including Ericsson, Philips, Samsung, SAP, and Sony Mobile. In most of these companies, these inner source programmes are initiated by one or a few 'champions,' the people who have a vision and "make it happen." The nine cues presented in this chapter provide a starting point for organizations that wish to adopt inner source. However, the field is still in its nascent phase, and there are numerous aspects of inner source that are not well understood. In this section we discuss a number of potential avenues for further research.

3.6.1 Managing Inner Source Projects

The way inner source projects are managed is very different from traditional software project management. This is necessarily so, because inner source projects, just like open source projects, depend heavily on the involvement of developers that select themselves to participate. In other words, nobody else tells them to participate. However, projects still must be managed; even open source projects do not survive without proper project management. Höst et al. (2014) explored inner source project management with two case studies and identified a number of tension points that managers should consider when they are involved in inner source projects. Gurbani et al. (2010) described a number of new roles that emerged in the inner source project at Bell Laboratories (Lucent). Besides the well known roles of 'Benevolent Dictator For Life' (BDFL) found in many open source projects, new roles included delivery advocate, feature advocate, release advocate, and that of a liaison who works with the various business units within an organization. Each of these roles assumes certain responsibilities to streamline the management of an inner source project. Besides these case studies, little is known about governance models in inner source projects; this is, however, an important area to study further in order to provide useful guidance to companies that wish to adopt inner source in a more strategic way.

3.6.2 Inner Source Adoption Models

The various organizations that have adopted inner source all do so in their own way, tailored to the context of an organization and the constraints an organization may be subject to (such as compliance with regulatory standards). Gurbani et al. (2010)

identified two main models of inner source adoption: project-specific inner source projects, and the infrastructure-based adoption model. In the former, a specific critical resource (a common but important software component) is managed by a development team and made available throughout the organization. The development team takes responsibility for the evolution and roadmap of the shared asset and can take in contributions from other developers in the organization. This model is appropriate if the shared asset is an important component to several divisions within an organization. This is the case for instance at Lucent, where the implementation of the Session Initiation Protocol (SIP) stack was "innersourced." Philips Healthcare has also adopted this model.

The second model is the infrastructure-based model, and does not focus specifically on a specific critical resource. Instead, the organization provides the necessary infrastructure to set up inner source projects, such as an internal SourceForge. Using this model, different divisions can decide for themselves which software components they would like to share throughout the organization and for which development is "opened up." This model tends to be the most common inner source model.

While this initial classification is a useful way to organize different inner source initiatives, it is at a very high level and does not provide insights into the more specific differences in how these initiatives are implemented. What is needed is an inner source taxonomy, a structure that can be used to organize and describe different initiatives at a detailed level. Furthermore, each inner source initiative is constrained by its context. For instance, Philips Healthcare develops medical systems and consequently these systems are subject to FDA regulation. This means that the production process (including that for the software) must be traceable. This will inevitably have consequences for the degree of "bazaar-style" practices that can be adopted. Insights into how different organizations have overcome their specific challenges are missing as of yet, and further research is needed to identify these mechanisms.

Chapter 4
Crowdsourcing

In this chapter we investigate the crowdsourcing phenomenon through a case study of a multinational company who embarked on a significant crowdsourcing software development initiative. Most studies aim to explain crowdsourcing by describing successful cases (e.g., Brabham 2008); as a result, there has been little attention to the challenges that may arise. Further research is therefore needed to better understand the limits of crowdsourcing software development. This chapter presents an in-depth industry case study of crowdsourcing software development at a multinational corporation. The goal is to shed light on the key issues in crowdsourcing that are relevant to software development. The study reveals a number of challenges that the case study organization encountered. In previous work (Stol and Fitzgerald 2014a, b), we drew on the crowdsourcing literature to synthesize a set of six cues which have particular relevance in a crowdsourcing software development context:

1. Task Decomposition
2. Coordination and Communication
3. Planning and Scheduling
4. Quality Assurance
5. Knowledge and Intellectual Property
6. Motivation and Remuneration

Details on the particular case study research methodology used in the study are provided in Stol and Fitzgerald (2014a, c).

This chapter is structured as follows. Sect. 4.1 provides some background on the company and describes the general case context. Sect. 4.2 uses the six cues identified to describe how their crowdsourcing software development experience played out.

© The Author(s) 2015
P.J. Ågerfalk et al., *Software Sourcing in the Age of Open*, SpringerBriefs
in Computer Science, DOI 10.1007/978-3-319-17266-8_4

4.1 Introduction to the Case Study

Tech Platform Inc. (TPI, a pseudonym) is a global player offering services and solutions in the cloud. The company employs about 50,000 people worldwide, with 400 sales offices, and partners in more than 75 countries. TPI sought to investigate the use of crowdsourcing in its software development function at the instigation of a senior executive.

The platform through which TPI chose to crowdsource its software development was TopCoder (TC), a proprietary crowdsourcing development platform which was acquired by Appirio in 2013, with the declared mission of providing *"enterprises with efficient access to the world's best technical talent."* TC is one of the largest software development crowdsourcing platforms, with its community having grown more than fourteen-fold, from 50,000 members in 2004 to more than 700,000 in 2014. However, an estimate in 2012 suggested that only 0.7 % of registered members had participated in software development.

TC has an extremely impressive customer list of blue chip companies and offers a platform which facilitates what is termed the three pillars of Digital Creation: (1) front-end innovation; (2) software development, and (3) algorithms and analytics. In this case study, we focused on the software development pillar.

TC accomplishes software development tasks for customers through a series of competitions. The TC community breaks down customer projects into atomized units of work that comprise the entire build, and these work units are accomplished through competitive contests, whereby the TC community compete and submit solutions. The TC community is structured into Program Managers who oversee customer projects and choose co-pilots within the TC community. These co-pilots act as an interface between customers and TC developers, and help rank submissions into winners (and runners-up) for the various contests.

Co-pilots are experienced TC community members who have proven themselves in the past on the TC platform. They manage the technical aspects of crafting and running competitions through to successful delivery. TC suggests that the co-pilots can do the technical heavy lifting and process management, allowing the customer to be the *"conductor of a world-wide talent pool."*[1]

The TC software development process comprises a number of different competition types, organized in a number of categories, as illustrated in Fig. 4.1.

The application which TPI selected for crowdsourcing was Titan, a web application to be used by TPI field engineers when migrating from one platform to another as part of a customer engagement. Within TPI a technical decision was taken that future development should use HTML5, and this was the technology chosen for the front end, which was replacing the desktop application. The back-end services were based on a similar technology set used by the previous desktop-based solution. TPI were keen to leverage HTML5 expertise from the large global TC community. Figure 4.2 illustrates the breakdown of the development work in terms of what was

---

[1] http://www.topcoder.com/whatiseoi/ (accessed 5 Oct 2012)

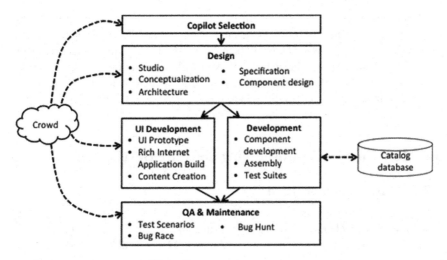

Fig. 4.1 The topcoder software development process

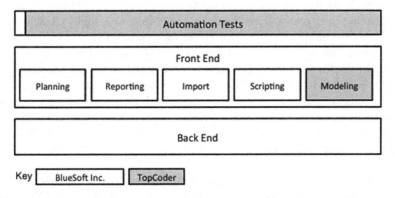

Fig. 4.2 Work decomposition between TC and TPI

to be done by TPI, and what was to be done by TopCoder. It should be noted that the dimensions of the figure do not reflect the actual amount of work. Given that a lot of TPI domain-specific knowledge is required for back-end development, this is retained as part of the TPI development responsibility.

Similarly in the front-end, topics such as migration planning, importing and the scripting engine were retained for development by TPI. The two activities that are part of the TC crowdsourced development are asset modeling and automation testing. Modeling refers to the arrays and switches that need to be migrated and thus have to be modeled (i.e., created and configured) in the Titan application. Automation testing complements unit and integration testing which is designed by TPI developers, and refers to the testing designed by QA to test the front-end GUI interaction with the back-end. As can be seen in Fig. 4.2, this development activity will be carried out almost entirely by TC. The small portion that will be developed by TPI involves a "Gold Standard" which will be made available subsequently as a template for the TC community to indicate how TPI would like automation testing to be done.

In Sect. 4.2 we use the six cues mentioned earlier to analyse the TC crowdsourcing development for the TPI web application.

4.2 Key Cues in Crowdsourcing Software Development

4.2.1 Task Decomposition

A key issue in crowdsourcing is that work is decomposed into a set of smaller tasks. In many crowdsourcing contexts, such as Amazon Mechanical Turk, tasks are usually small and largely independent. However, in contrast, software development tasks are typically more complex and interdependent. What is of particular importance, given the interdependencies in software, is that different developers working on a project know how their code fits into the resulting software product, in terms of understanding interfaces and assumptions made. Therefore, a key challenge is to find an appropriate decomposition of the software product into tasks that can be effectively crowdsourced. Indeed, better decompositions can lead to an increased parallelism (LaToza et al. 2013). Further, Tajedin and Nevo (2013) suggest that projects which can be decomposed into small modules with clear requirements and limited interdependencies are more likely to succeed. However, when decomposing a software development task, a balance needs to be struck between providing a sufficiently detailed specification for the task being crowdsourced on the one hand, and stifling innovation with overly detailed specifications on the other hand (Lakhani et al. 2010).

The choice as to what parts of the product were appropriate for crowdsourcing was not entirely trivial for TPI. Code and executables which were self-contained would be easier to merge and hence were more suitable for crowdsourcing. However, if code from TC had to be directly merged with code being developed in-house, this would be more problematic. The decision as to what work to crowdsource was primarily based on internal resources (or lack thereof) and the amount of domain knowledge required for a certain task. Tasks that required the least amount of domain knowledge were deemed most suitable.

TPI divided the project into five development phases, listed in Table 4.1. The first dashboards phase was the front-end which involved the high-level dashboard interface pages, e.g., for customer creation, project creation and navigation. The next two development phases involved configuration of TPI's flagship product. Following this, Phase 4 was concerned with the various network devices which also formed part of the migration configuration. Finally, Phase 5 dealt with the low-end legacy products and various third party solutions that also needed to be migrated. In order to minimize the modifications that would need to be made to the TC code after delivery, TPI made the header and footer browser code available to TC developers.

Table 4.1 Titan development phases and specifications

Phase	Description	Panels	Documents	Pages
1	Dashboards	40	NA	NA
2	Flagship product I	18	15	196
3	Flagship product II	33	19	543
4	Network devices	14	11	161
5	Legacy and third-party	23	17	131

This was to ensure this standard format would be maintained by all TC developers. For the Titan application, TPI's policy was to only use HTML5 where a feature was supported by all platforms to increase portability. Initially, there was an expectation that the TC community would deliver some innovative HTML5 code. However, the TPI requirement that HTML5 features would have to be supported by all browser platforms resulted in a very small proportion of all potential HTML5 features being available for use by TC developers. The expected innovation from the "crowd" was thus precluded by the TPI specification.

In order to minimize integration effort later on, TPI had wanted to let TC developers work against a real back-end core as opposed to stub services. However, at the time development with TC started, the core was not ready and stubs were used during most development contests. Consequently, this integration effort was pushed back to a later stage in the development process, which was not ideal.

For traditional in-house development, TPI developers had internalized a great deal of information in relation to coding standards and templates, and technical specifications. However, many of the coding standards and templates were documented informally and not stored centrally on the internal wiki installation. This scattering of information and URLs prevented it from being packaged as a deliverable for TC developers. TPI had to undertake a great deal of extra work to ensure that this information was made explicit in the requirements specification for the external TC developers. Most of the effort was related to the technical specifications. Table 4.1 above lists the number of documents (62) and the total number of pages of specifications (1,031 pages) written for each of the five development phases defined by TPI. The architect liaising with TC described the situation as follows:

> It feels like we've produced a million specification documents, but obviously we haven't. The way we do specifications for TopCoder is entirely different to how we do them internally.

4.2.2   Coordination and Communication

Malone and Crowston (1994) defined coordination as *"the process of managing dependencies among activities."* As such, coordination is concerned with directing efforts of individuals toward a common and explicitly recognized goal, and linking different parts of an organization together to achieve a set of tasks (Kraut and

Streeter 1995). Although related to task decomposition discussed above, coordination is specifically concerned with communication, interdependencies and integrating various parts into a whole (Kraut and Streeter 1995; LaToza et al. 2013). When crowdsourcing more complex tasks, as is the case in software development, there is a need for coordination (Kittur et al. 2013).

The above characterization of coordination is implicitly based on the assumption that activities are conducted within an organization. Clearly, in crowdsourcing, participants are not part of the crowdsourcing customer organization. In fact, interdependent tasks may be performed by different workers, potentially causing incompatibilities between the solutions provided (LaToza et al. 2013).

In a software engineering context, the need for different developers to communicate is often related to Brooks' Law ("adding manpower to a late software project makes it later"), in that the more people involved, the higher the communication overhead (Brooks 1995). In a crowdsourcing context, communication needs are greater in the requirements specification and solution validation phases, whereas during the actual competition phases, as is the case with TC, there is unlikely to be any communication between developers since they are competing against each other.

From the TC perspective, the software development process consisted of a number of interrelated phases (see Fig. 4.1 above). While the TC process was essentially a waterfall one, an agile development process, based on Scrum, was in use at TPI. Synthesizing these different development processes was problematic. TC development had to be assigned to a Scrum team within TPI, and TC contributions needed to be subsequently injected into the appropriate sprints. A TPI architect summarized the central problem as follows:

> We are an agile shop and we are used to changing our minds. This can be a problem with TC when we tell them one thing in one contest, but have changed our mind in the next contest.

There were also quite a number of layers in the engagement model between TC and TPI. Firstly at the TC end, a co-pilot liaised between the TC developer community on the one hand, and TPI personnel on the other hand. Furthermore, a platform specialist and the TPI account manager were involved, effectively overseeing the co-pilot and recommending changes at that level.

Within TPI, the choice of personnel to interact with the TC co-pilot was a difficult decision. While TC would prefer a single point of contact within the customer organization, there were significant management and technical issues involved, thus requiring senior people from TPI on both the management and technical end. A senior TC program manager was appointed specifically for all programs being developed with TC. This manager ensured that management were aware of any scheduling issues that could arise, for example, and also ensured that training was provided. However, there was also a specific Titan program manager, and thus there was inevitably some overlap between both roles. On the technical side at TPI, a senior architect was allocated to coordinate the TC development for the Titan project. This role of TC liaison, which involved daily contact with the TC community, was considered to be problematic within TPI, given the considerable pressure to answer questions which was also very time consuming. There was some concern within TPI about allocating such a senior resource to this liaison role given the significant cost. The Software Development Manager described the situation from a resource allocation perspective:

> To have a single point of contact for the project on our side, the contact needs to have both technical skills and project management skills to be able to manage the requirements, competitions and questions from TopCoder technical community members. It used a very valuable resource and in this project they had to use up some time from other developers to address all the questions coming back from TopCoder.

At the initial stage, this liaison role involved answering questions on the TC Forums. There was significant time pressure involved since a time penalty would be incurred if forum questions were not answered in a timely fashion by TPI, which would mean that the original committed delivery date for TC development would be pushed out. Also, the architect estimated the time answering questions on the TC Forums to be at least twice as long as would be the case with internal development:

> There are a lot more questions than with internal development. However, there is no informal communication mechanism. You cannot yell at the person in the next cubicle and get the answer very quickly.

A sense of 'belonging' to the same team, or the development of 'teamness,' has been found to be an important factor in distributed development (Carmel 1999; Lings et al. 2007). However, in this case of crowdsourcing, the only relationship which tended to build over time was that with the TC copilot. There was no real opportunity to build up a relationship with any of the TC developers, as interaction was filtered through a number of layers. Another structural coordination issue arose in that TPI allocated architects to products, and the desire to get the TC project completed resulted in two additional architects working on the project. This was seen as a sub-optimal resource allocation, given that the architect role was a somewhat scarce and extremely valuable resource.

TPI also had a so-called "tactical" Scrum team that could be assigned to different tasks more flexibly in that this team was not formally assigned to projects on a long-term basis, as was the case with the other Scrum teams at TPI. The tactical team could deal with TC contributions when they arrived. However, in some cases a normal Scrum team would also be assigned to the project, and in these cases involvement of the tactical Scrum team would not then be necessary. Overall, there was extra overhead and duplication of work on the project in that two teams had to become familiar with the project and its deliverables. These two teams also had to communicate with each other. To address this issue, TPI dropped the use of the tactical team, and instead scheduled time in regular project sprints to integrate the deliveries from TC.

4.2.3   Planning and Scheduling

With crowdsourcing, one or more tasks are typically given to an unknown workforce to complete, and as a result an organization is letting go of control of that particular work. On the one hand, this can result in timely delivery of completed work since it can be completed in parallel and independently of the organization's in-house workforce. Particularly if the tasks involve competitions where payment depends on timely delivery. On the other hand, this introduces a level of uncertainty as to whether or not the work will be completed on time (Zhao and Zhu 2012). One of the expected benefits of crowdsourcing is that of shortening the product development cycle (Brabham 2008; Vukovic 2009). In order to achieve this, it is important that the desired schedule of a crowdsourcing organization can be adhered to by the crowd. For instance, a core challenge is to ensure that sufficient workers are available when needed. While there may be extensive expertise within the crowd, very specific domain knowledge may not always be available at the moment it is needed. Furthermore, it is important to ensure that sufficient time is given to coders, relating the issue of planning to the size and scope of a task. Lakhani et al. (2010) reported that TopCoder "*community members worked best when contests lasted less than 2 weeks.*" Projects which are too large or long-lasting can result in decreased interest from the community, and thus fewer submissions.

The Titan project comprised more than fifty TC competitions. These competitions involved a total of 695 contest days, with an average length of competition of just over 13 days. The shortest completion time for a competition was 4 days while the longest competition took 32 days to complete. As discussed above, TPI had structured the overall development of the Titan product into five phases. The average duration across these development phases is 80 days, with the longest development duration (90 days) for the front-end HTML5 panels in the first phase, and the shortest development duration (69 days) for the final phase involving the low-end legacy and third-party arrays. Table 4.2 lists the duration of each phase, the number of competitions per phase, and the average length of a competition per phase. (Note that in practice, competitions overlap so that the duration of a phase is not merely the number of competitions times their length.)

Some of the specific timings and the granularity of possible decisions for TC development were somewhat problematic for TPI. For example, TC allows a customer 5 days to accept or reject a deliverable. According to the architect, this was often not long enough to analyze and fully test the deliverable, and it was difficult to get these reviews done in time internally. A further difficulty arose in that TC deliverables had to be accepted as a whole, or rejected as a whole, with no middle ground. It would have been better from TPI's point of view if more flexible granularity was possible in that certain parts of deliverables could be accepted and partial payment made for these acceptable parts. Because TPI did not want to deter TC

Table 4.2 Development phases and document specifications

Phase	Description	Panels	Documents	Pages
1	Dashboards	40	NA	NA
2	Flagship product I	18	15	196
3	Flagship product II	33	19	543
4	Network devices	14	11	161
5	Legacy and third-party	23	17	131

developers from bidding on future competitions, there was a tendency to accept submissions, even with some defects. TC offer an additional warranty period of 30 days, but integrating fixes under this warranty would pose considerable overhead in receiving, checking and integrating new code with an active code base which would more than likely have undergone significant further modification internally within TPI in the interim. Furthermore, when issues were escalated within the 30-day warranty, the resolutions were generally not satisfactory to TPI. Overall, a single longer initial acceptance period of 15 days would probably be more beneficial to TPI than the two current periods of 5 and 30 days, respectively. Another issue related to planning and scheduling arose when TPI had to wait for a contest to finish, while the main application was evolving, causing possible integration issues. TPI's schedule was also jeopardized by several contests failing due to a lack of submissions. These contests had to be rescheduled thus causing a delay in TPI's schedule. When rescheduled, there was only a single submission in one contest, despite more than 30 registrants indicating an interest.

As already discussed, TPI felt the need to run multiple competitions in parallel so as to shorten the development time, and therefore chose to run development phases concurrently. However, this clearly had implications for coordination. For example, there were interdependencies between the products produced in the various development phases. This also led to duplication of functionality in the JSP and CSS code.

4.2.4   Quality Assurance

Another claim made by crowdsourcing advocates is that the quality of submissions is high (Bonabeau 2009; Schenk and Guittard 2011). However, there is a risk of 'noise' in submissions, which can result in solutions being of low quality (Dow et al. 2012; Ipeirotis and Paritosh 2011). As noted in earlier chapters, in a software development context, the idea that involving a wide variety of developers helps in finding and fixing defects is better known as Linus's Law, or, "*given enough eyeballs, all bugs are shallow*" (Raymond 2001). Closely related to this is the idea that there is a wide variety of expertise within a developer community. The challenge lies in attracting sufficient contestants, under the assumption that given enough contestants, the required expertise will be present. Whereas AMT is non-transparent, in that contestants do not know how many 'competitors' there are for a certain competition, a platform such as TopCoder is fully transparent. Prior to participating, contestants must register for a certain competition. Findings from a recent study suggest, however, that the greater the number of contest participants, the lower the quality of the work (Kinnaird et al. 2013). One characteristic sometimes ascribed to the crowd is that it consists mostly of amateurs (Schenk and Guittard 2011), thus suggesting that the resulting quality of output may not be on par with professional work. However, Brabham (2012) argues that this is a myth.

Quality assurance is a key concern in software development, whether the software is developed in-house or by external parties. Of particular concern in crowdsourcing is that a customer has no knowledge of the developers that deliver the software, nor of the process that they might follow, and therefore has no control of these aspects. Crowd developers may "*satisfice, minimizing the amount of effort they expend*" (Kittur et al. 2013). Also, there can be disagreement about a solution; Kittur (2010) distinguished 'subjective' tasks for which there is no single right answer, and 'objective' tasks that can easily be verified. Although software either fulfills a set of requirements or not, disagreements may still arise regarding certain functionality or the scope of a task. Furthermore, quality attributes of submissions, such as performance and maintainability of the code may still vary. One approach to quality control is peer-review. At TopCoder, for instance, members of the community perform peer-reviews of the submitted software. Similar to peer-reviews in open source, such reviews are "truly independent" (Feller and Fitzgerald 2002) given that the peer-reviewers would usually not know the creator of the work, and would therefore unlikely be biased. A certain level of 'shepherding' the crowd has also been suggested to improve quality (Kulkarni et al. 2012). Kulkarni et al. (2012) found that letting the crowd plan amongst themselves without supervision of a requester was partially successful, but that intervention by a requester during the workflow could improve quality significantly.

Much research in software engineering has focused on identifying and eliminating errors as early as possible in the development process, on the well established basis that errors cost exponentially more to rectify, the later they are found in the development cycle (Boehm, 1981). However, the structure of the TC development process made it difficult to preserve this, as it shifted QA issues towards later stages of the development process, after coding has been completed. As the Development Manager expressed it:

> Crowdsourcing focuses on requirements and relaxes the quality process at the onset of the project, so now all the emphasis on managing the quality comes at the QA cycles later in the project, and that tends to be more expensive

The number of defects identified was quite significant—506 bugs were identified in the 128 HTML5 panels. While many issues were of a cosmetic nature, and therefore fairly trivial, the sheer volume of issues required considerable time and attention from developers within TPI. Furthermore, as more contests were finished and software delivered back to TPI, the rate of new issues was increasing as well.

There was also a problem with lack of continuity. TC developers do not remain idle at the end of competitions, and may thus not be free to continue with TPI development in subsequent tasks. In fact, TPI experienced problems with bugs which had previously been identified being re-introduced to code after it went back for further development with TC. This added to the critical perception expressed by the Divisional CTO, who characterised crowdsourcing as being "a fleeting relationship" in contrast to the investment one would be prepared to make when using remote development teams for development.

Given that the combination of technical and specific domain expertise was considered by TPI to be quite rare (based on experience in recruiting developers), TPI took some initiatives to improve the quality of crowdsourced contributions. For example, a virtual machine with a sample core application was made available as an image that could easily be downloaded and run. This was used by the TC development community both in development and as a final test or demonstrator for code they developed. Prior to this, TC code testing was done with stubbed-out service calls to the back-end, but there was a concern within TPI that TC code would not necessarily run smoothly when connected fully to the back-end. When the code for the initial HTML5 high-level panel applications was produced by TC, there were some quality issues, for instance, the same header was repeated in every file. TPI took this code and further developed it to a "Gold Standard," at the level required by TPI. This was delivered back to the TC community as a template for future development. This tactic was extended to prepare sample code for a web application that could act as a template for the TC community. This included a parent project object model (build script), source code compliant with all TPI code standards, unit and integration tests, automation tests, and instructions for deployment and setup.

4.2.5 Knowledge and Intellectual Property

Knowledge management has long been recognized to be an important topic within the software engineering field (Aurum et al. 2003; Bjørnson and Dingsøyr 2008). A key difference between crowdsourcing and traditional outsourcing is that there is no single supplier that develops an in-depth understanding of the problem domain of a crowdsourced project; rather, the continuous turnover of workers is an inherent characteristic of crowdsourcing (Dabbish et al. 2012).

One significant knowledge issue of particular concern in crowdsourcing software development tasks has to do with intellectual property (IP). IP 'leakage' and the consequent loss of competitive advantage is a challenge in adopting crowdsourcing. Organizations may be hesitant to provide too many details on a certain task (i.e., module or component) that is crowdsourced, yet sufficient detail in the specification is necessary for developers in the crowd to understand what the crowdsourcing organization is requesting. Another issue that may arise is IP ownership. Tasks on general-purpose platforms such as AMT are arguably relatively simple (requiring little human intelligence), and thus IP concerns do not loom large. Software development, however, is a highly creative process, and organizations will want to ensure they can patent any potential inventions that emerge with no confusion in relation to ownership. A third issue can arise when workers submit solutions that are not free and unencumbered, for instance, if the solution contains open source code with the restrictive GNU Public License (GPL) license. This may be a risk for crowdsourcing customers as it affects their product.

The "fleeting relationship" mentioned earlier also has consequences for knowledge management and IP at TPI. According to the architect involved in the project, the lack of depth in the relationship with contestants meant that:

> there is a limited amount of carry-over knowledge. We will get a few contestants that will participate in multiple contests, but they won't build up domain knowledge in the way that an internal person would.

Also, given that there is no single supplier as would be the case in a traditional outsourcing scenario, any intellectual property relating to specifications and product knowledge is more widely exposed simply by virtue of its being viewed by the 'crowd' of potential developers. Table 4.3 shows the total number of registrants, and the total number of submissions per contest type. The table shows that there were considerable numbers of potential participants (each of whom would have access to the contest specifications), but that the number of submissions was significantly lower—almost 90 % of those registered for a contest did not actually submit anything to that contest. In other words, making detailed product and specification information available, which is necessary to achieve the benefit of tapping into the crowd's wisdom and creativity, seems (in this case) not to be as fruitful as one would hope given the limited numbers of submissions.

TPI chose a pseudonym to disguise their participation on the TC platform. This was to obfuscate the fact that the work was for the TPI platform as it was felt that developers from competing organizations might be working for TC in their spare time. TPI took advantage of the standard Competition Confidentiality Agreement (CCA) which TC use with their development community. TPI will not do business with certain countries, for example, and this can be policed through the CCA which identifies the home location of TC developers. TPI were still concerned about the extent to which proprietary information could be exposed in TC competitions. To address this, TPI plan to identify the "Secret Sauce" which should not be shared without very careful consideration. This would include the source code for the flagship and legacy applications, libraries and binaries from other TPI business units, performance calculation formulae, hardware specifications and business rules.

Table 4.3 Number of registered contestants and submissions per contest type

Type	Registrants	Submissions
Copilot	13	6
Studio	34	7
Architecture	90	12
Assembly	476	36
Test Suite	8	1
UI Prototype	99	22
Total	**720**	**84**

4.2.6   Motivation and Remuneration

A final consideration in crowdsourcing is that of motivation and remuneration. Motivation is a topic that has received considerable attention in the software engineering research field, given that it is reported to be a major factor in project success (Beecham et al. 2008; Boehm 1981). Motivational factors can be intrinsic or extrinsic. Intrinsic motivation refers to internal motivation that is derived from an individual's pure interest or enjoyment in the task itself (e.g., having fun, gaining recognition and a sense of achievement). Extrinsic motivation, on the other hand, arises when an activity is driven by the desire to receive a reward, typically a payment, or to win a competition. Such motivation is generally external to the individual.

Obviously, the compensation of a certain crowdsourcing task will depend heavily on the expected duration and the complexity of the task. Tasks can vary in complexity, from so-called 'micro-tasks,' such as tagging an image which takes only seconds, to more time-consuming tasks such as transcribing audio. Clearly, software development tasks are complex and time-consuming, and contestants will expect significant remuneration, as opposed to the average cost of micro-tasks on AMT, most of which are below one US dollar (Ipeirotis 2010). One benefit of crowdsourcing is that it can greatly reduce cost. Yet, determining an appropriate price is a key challenge for crowdsourcing in general, and also for software development specifically (Lakhani et al. 2010).

Given a potential development community in excess of 700,000 members, TC would claim to have broad and deep enough expertise to ensure a healthy competition rate. However, TPI have had to cancel some competitions because of a lack of participation and there had been a number of others with just a single contestant. The fact that TPI used a pseudonym does appear to be significant in that well known companies do attract TC developers more readily and TPI would certainly be a very well known company globally. The TC pricing structure was quite complex. At the top level, there was a monthly platform fee to TC. For TPI this was a monthly fee of $30,000. This allowed access to the TC component catalog containing more than 1,500 software solutions. TC estimates that approximately 60 % of client projects can be solved through reusing components from this catalog. However, TPI were not in a position to leverage this catalog, since a lot of their IT product stack has already been developed, as the software development manager explained:

> We have our technology stack built and a lot of our software is already written for that. So the TopCoder catalog is not much use to us. There's no real bang for the buck for us there.

The co-pilot who was the principal liaison between TC and TPI typically cost $600 per contest. There was an initial specification review before the contest begins, and this cost $50. The individual contest pricing was also quite complex. In the case of TPI, first prizes for contests ranged from $200 up to $2,400, depending on the size and complexity of a contest. A second prize of 50 % of the first prize was paid to the runner up in each contest, but this prize would *only* be paid if the quality rating of the submission were at least 75 (out of 100). If this score were less than 75, the runner-up would only receive Digital Run points (discussed below).

There was also a Reliability Bonus which was paid to the winning submission. The calculation of this bonus is quite detailed, but basically it can be up to 20 % of the first prize, depending on the past successful track record of the winning contestant (i.e., his/her reliability—does a contestant actually submit after registering?). In addition, there was a cost of 45 % of the first prize to support the TC Digital Run, an initiative whereby TC share money with the TC development community based on the monthly contest revenue and proportional to the number of points that TC developers have amassed in contests. The Digital Run is an additional mechanism to motivate potential contestants to participate even if they assess their chance of winning to be low. Following the contests, three reviewers from the TC community evaluated submissions and this cost approximately $800 on average. Finally, TC charged a 100 % commission equal to the total development costs above. Overall, the total average cost per competition so far was approximately $7,200 (excluding the monthly platform fee).

In comparison with traditional development in-house, the Program Manager was of the opinion that TC development was less effective due to the lack of domain knowledge of the crowd and the indirect nature of the communication with developers. The primary reason for working with TC was the need to get development done more rapidly than would be possible with the existing level of internal resources. However, given the planning and schedule figures above, it is clear that the expectations in relation to a more rapid development time-frame were not fully realized.

4.3 Summary of Key Crowdsourcing Findings

Crowdsourcing software development is a distinct and emerging approach to software development. Contrary to traditional outsourcing strategies that are characterized by contracts between two parties—the customer and supplier—crowdsourcing introduces a third party of unknown magnitude (sometimes very small in fact) and diversity, namely the crowd. Rather than a single supplier, there can be any number of contributors. This has clear implications for the six cues identified above, namely task decomposition, coordination and communication, planning and scheduling, QA, knowledge and IP, and motivation and remuneration (Table 4.4).

Table 4.4 Key findings for the crowdsourcing cues

Task decomposition	
• Three important factors to consider when deciding what to crowdsource	
o Least business domain knowledge required	
o Scarce internal resources	
o Self-contained work to ease subsequent re-integration	
Coordination and communication	
• Multiple interaction layers	
• High degree of overhead and duplication of work roles	
• Coordination/quality issues arise in reconciling the waterfall-style development process which crowdsourcing represents with the agile development process more commonly practiced in organizations now	
Planning and scheduling	
• Many contests may be necessary to get work done	
• Some contests may need to be repeated if no submissions	
• Five-day and 30-day warranty periods problematic	
Quality assurance	
• Quality is affected negatively as error detection is delayed later than typical best practice	
• Fleeting relationship as developers not working on subsequent contests so error tend to recur	
Knowledge and intellectual property	
• Not much innovation as the 'Crowd' may be very small indeed	
• Unknown workforce may be seeing the organisation's "secret sauce"	
Motivation and remuneration	
• Can be very expensive when all the platform charges are taken into account	
• Extrinsic motivation as contestants tend to withdraw if they perceive their chances of winning as low	

4.4 Implications for Research and Practice

Crowdsourcing is an emerging topic and several benefits have been identified in Chap. 1. Research suggests that crowdsourcing can be a viable option in a variety of situations, but very few studies so far have focused on crowdsourcing in a software development context.

The TopCoder crowdsourcing platform represents a significant 'market' of supply and demand for software development tasks. TopCoder claims many benefits can be achieved in terms of quality, cost, speed and flexibility (Lakhani et al. 2010). However, the results of our study suggest that these benefits are not easy or automatic to realize. The TPI case identifies a number of significant challenges that the company had not foreseen prior to embarking on the crowdsourcing approach.

In relation to the basic issues of cost, time and quality, while we do not yet have a definitive direct comparison with a similar development project done in-house, it is certainly the case that the TPI development staff are not convinced that the TC model offers clear advantages in relation to cost, time and quality.

While the amount of work to be done by TC developers represented a significant part of the whole project, the complexity of the UI panels is arguably simple, in that it does not require significant business domain knowledge. Yet, TPI spent significant time and effort on writing specification documentation, much more so than if the software was being developed internally. This TPI internal effort has not been factored directly into the costs incurred, nor has any of the subsequent interaction and coordination effort of TPI personnel. The time-scale for this development work was of considerable magnitude, as discussed in Sect. 4.2.3. However, it is particularly difficult to make precise effort estimates for a crowdsourced project: it is not possible to determine the actual effort spent by TC developers on a contest. There is a fixed end date for contests regardless of when contestants actually finish the work involved. Furthermore, in the (quite common) case of multiple contestants, efforts will vary across contestants, and some contestants may start on a submission but not finish. Also, comparing TC development effort with in-house development is complicated due to varying factors, such as the overhead imposed on TC developers to understand the context of the work at hand. Finally, in relation to quality, even though the front-end development done by the crowd was of relatively low complexity.

An important consideration also is that TC's formulation of the software development process is effectively a waterfall approach, despite widely accepted wisdom that the waterfall model is not well suited to the rapid pace of change in modern development contexts. Agile and iterative methods are becoming increasingly popular in industry, including in domains where they have long been considered unsuitable (Fitzgerald et al. 2013), suggesting that these methods offer significant benefits over the waterfall model. The waterfall process also has serious consequences in that quality assurance practices are pushed to the end of the development process. While this can partly be addressed by adding a requirement to include unit tests, integration of the task is still done at a later stage, after a competition has finished.

Overall, TPI are of the opinion that crowdsourcing is limited in the areas in which it is suitable. Areas such as storyboards, GUI design, and even icon design, worked well for TPI. These areas seem to be quite self-contained without interdependencies. However, when there were dependencies between deliverables, and back and forth communication was necessary, the situation was quite different. Crowdsourcing competitions are effectively 'black-boxed,' meaning that while a competition is ongoing, a customer has limited means to communicate with TC developers. While there can be frequent communication with contestants prior to commencement of a contest, once it starts, communication is through a co-pilot, who acts as a proxy and thus represents an additional interaction layer.

The results and insights of this case study suggest a number of open questions that we believe need further attention. Contestants who are not familiar with the TopCoder software development process may not be as successful as other contestants who have extensive experience with the process. The duration of TPI's engagement with TC has been less than a year, and some of the challenges encountered may have been due to this lack of experience. Thus, one significant contribution to software engineering research would be to conduct longitudinal studies of organizations that have used a crowdsourcing approach for software development.

Chapter 5
Conclusion

The previous three chapters presented different forms of software outsourcing to an unknown workforce—opensourcing, innersourcing and crowdsourcing. These sourcing strategies all rely on a workforce that is not fully known in advance, unlike conventional software projects where teams are formed before a project is started. Furthermore, there are varying degrees of 'unknownness.' In opensourcing, it could be very hard to identify the actual people who are working on the software, as developers may operate under an alias. In innersourcing, it is not known in advance who will be working on the software, but it will be much easier to identify who the contributors are, as they will use their corporate identity (their corporate email address, for instance). In crowdsourcing, it will be possible to identify the developers 'after the fact.' That is, once a crowdsourcing contest comes to its end and the 'winner' is selected, his or her identity will be known.

Each form of software sourcing presented in this book is appropriate for some situations, and less so for others. They differ in a number of ways, which is why each chapter drew on a different set of factors or issues that was of particular relevance for the respective strategy. However, in order to compare the three strategies and provide concrete guidance to software managers as to which strategy should be pursued, we developed a comparison framework. This chapter presents this framework; for each comparison criterion, we discuss the implications for each sourcing strategy.

5.1 A Comparison Framework

The three alternative strategies for outsourcing that were presented in Chaps. 2 to 4 differ in a number of significant ways. In this section we discuss a number of dimensions along which these alternative forms of outsourcing differ. Table 5.1 below illustrates how these three forms of open-source inspired sourcing differ from outsourcing and from each other.

© The Author(s) 2015
P.J. Ågerfalk et al., *Software Sourcing in the Age of Open*, SpringerBriefs
in Computer Science, DOI 10.1007/978-3-319-17266-8_5

Table 5.1 Comparison of outsourcing, opensourcing, innersourcing and crowdsourcing

	Outsourcing	Opensourcing	Innersourcing	Crowdsourcing
Locus of control	• Company • IP protected	• Community • IP open	• Company or Community • IP protected	• Company • IP protected
Nature of workforce	• Known • Narrow and deep knowledge	• Unknown, can be difficult to find out • Broad and deep knowledge	• Known • Broad and deep knowledge	• Unknown but known to platform • Broad and deep knowledge
Community motivation	• Extrinsic	• Intrinsic and extrinsic	• Extrinsic and intrinsic	• Extrinsic
Company motivation	• Resource saving • Overcoming lack of resources	• Innovation • Market growth • Cost sharing • Save resources (commodification)	• Reuse • Resource saving • Innovation	• Resource saving/ overcoming lack of resources • Innovation
Duration of engagement	Project-specific, contractual commitment	Prolonged commitment	Prolonged commitment	Ad hoc commitment
Nature of participation	Collaborative	Co-opetive	Collaborative	Competitive, possibly collaborative

5.1.1   Locus of Control

The locus of control refers to the question of who initiates and retains control in the sourcing relationship. In conventional software outsourcing, the locus of control lies with the customer company who has a certain software development task that is given to a third party to perform. In such an arrangement, one company (the customer) commissions another company (the provider) to perform the work. In this relationship, the customer takes the initiative and retains control by requesting specific and well specified tasks to be carried out by the provider. The resulting deliverable (i.e., the software produced by the provider) becomes the intellectual property of the paying customer.

Although a company engaging in opensourcing may ideally want to steer the long-term direction of a project, the locus of control will often lie primarily with the community. It was clear in the case of opensourcing that the customer could not dominate or control the agenda as this would lead to push-back from the community. The resulting deliverable from opensourcing (i.e., the software produced) will typically be released under an open source license and intellectual property will usually be shared openly. Alternatively, a company may opt for a dual licensing model and thus retain some control and flexibility in relation to the IP (as was the case in the Celtix project, for example (Ågerfalk and Fitzgerald 2008)).

Both innersourcing and opensourcing refers to the adoption of open source development philosophy by a commercial company. However, in terms of locus of control, innersourcing is pretty much a hybrid of opensourcing and outsourcing. Most cases of innersourcing start out as grassroots initiatives, suggesting that the locus of control lies with the (internal) 'community,' i.e., the developers employed by an organization (Stol et al. 2014). Innersourcing differs from opensourcing in that developers cannot completely ignore their position as a paid employee of the company or the job requirements of their position within that company. Different inner source projects that can be observed in practice have different governance models. For instance, the inner source initiative within Philips Healthcare has augmented the traditional governance model, by providing mechanisms and conventions that prescribe how contributions can be made and who is responsible for the maintenance of such contributions. This is necessary given the critical role that the shared asset plays as the platform that underpins the product line of medical devices, which are subject to regulatory authorities such as the FDA. Other inner source initiatives are more reminiscent of open source projects, whereby the locus of control lies with the 'community.' For example, a different inner source initiative within Philips Research (a different division of the Philips consortium) does not have formal leadership but rather a de-facto leadership that lies with the initiators of the project. Other companies may have different models of governance, and the development of a governance taxonomy of inner source projects is one area that we believe needs more research.

In terms of locus of control, crowdsourcing is very much along the lines of outsourcing. The customer company specifies the task to be done by the crowd community. This is decomposed into competitions under which community participants submit proposed solutions. Any IP is owned by the company. Although crowdsourcing is open source inspired, it departs significantly from open source principles. Companies use the crowd to reduce costs or to stimulate innovation through fresh and new ways of considering situations afforded by the crowd. However, the business model requires that the company control the situation.

5.1.2 Nature of Workforce

The nature of the workforce can be characterized by two factors: the degree of 'unknownness' and the nature of the knowledge that the workforce has.

In conventional outsourcing, the workforce is necessarily known; that is, an organization will choose a supplier on the basis of their known track record and ability to deliver, and a contract will have been put in place before any of the work is started. The level of expertise by the workforce of a known outsourcing supplier is typically narrow and deep. It is narrow because an outsourcing supplier may focus on a specific domain or certain technologies. However, given this specialization, the level of knowledge can be very deep.

In opensourcing, the identities of contributing developers are typically not known, although contributors may be asked to sign a contribution agreement,[1] thus providing their real name and signature. In a sense, the company outsources to a largely unknown workforce. The outsourcing model thus assumes that the collective of developers (i.e., the community) will deliver and does not tie compensation and rewards to individual contributions. By tapping into a large pool of developers, possibly spread across the globe, a company may get access to expertise that they would not have access to otherwise.

In contrast to opensourcing, in an inner source context, contributors will be known. User accounts (e.g., for commit access) are typically linked to developers' unique corporate email addresses. While developers within the same inner source project may have never met before (not uncommon in large distributed organizations), each member of the inner source project community will have a 'base' position in the company's hierarchy. With respect to the knowledge of the workforce, however, inner source is very similar to open source, in that an inner source project may benefit from a wide variety of contributors from throughout the company with very specific and deep knowledge.

In crowdsourcing, developers who participate in a contest are unknown to a customer (Stol and Fitzgerald 2014a). While different platforms exist for crowdsourcing, on the platform in the study we presented in Chap. 4, TopCoder, developers go by a nickname, or 'handle.' While developers need to specify certain information in order to get paid when winning a contest, very little information is public, except for the country in which a developer is based. This is necessary as a customer may choose to exclude submissions from certain countries. Furthermore, one of the problems that our crowdsourcing study revealed was the lack of continuity—the "fleeting relationship" in that developers in the crowd would not tend to wait for further competitions from a particular company but would work on whatever competitions were open. Also, customer companies may choose to remain anonymous on the TopCoder platform. This creates a two-way level of unknownness as neither customer nor community know who each other is in some cases.

With respect to the level of knowledge of the workforce, crowdsourcing is very similar to opensourcing and innersourcing, in that the degree of knowledge tends to be broad and deep for similar reasons as in opensourcing and innersourcing. If the available talent-pool is truly global, then there is good reason to expect broad and deep knowledge on the topics under development.

5.1.3   Community Motivation

The motivation of the developer community varies across the different sourcing strategies. In Chap. 4 above, we drew the distinction between intrinsic and extrinsic motivation. Intrinsic motivation refers to internal motivation that is derived from an individual's pure interest or enjoyment in the task itself. Extrinsic motivation, on

---

[1] http://en.wikipedia.org/wiki/Contributor_License_Agreement

the other hand, arises when an activity is driven by the desire to receive a reward, typically a payment, or to win a competition. Such motivation is generally external to the individual.

In the outsourcing context, the community or supplier motivation is clearly extrinsic. Suppliers perform a task for payment under a contract typically with penalties for late or non-performance.

Lerner and Tirole (2002) argued that the two major motivations for contributing to open source projects are career concerns and ego gratification, which they collectively referred to as the signaling incentive. By contributing to an open source project, developers gain reputation and status within that community, which thus appears to be the main driving force. This is echoed by Nov (2007) who studied incentives to contribute to Wikipedia based on Clary et al.'s (1998) motivational categories in volunteer work. Thus, the reward can be a delayed signaling incentive where successful open source developers could be rewarded eventually by better job prospects. In opensourcing, payment is sometimes part of the picture and developers may find a more direct link between their 'voluntary' work and potential career advancements than in traditional open source. Interestingly, this appears to be evolving as Riehle et al. (2014) reported that more than 50 % of open source code contributions occurred during office hours which suggests a conventional paid workforce, at least to some extent. This is in contrast to the earlier finding by Lakhani and Wolf (2005) whose large-scale survey found that only 40 % of open source developers were in organizations.

Motivation of developers in an innersourcing context can be either extrinsic or intrinsic. Typically, setting up an inner source initiative is not done at the request of a manager or supervisor, but rather these are often set up by visionary individuals. Contributors likewise may derive enjoyment and satisfaction from contributing to a project. On the other hand, external 'rewards' may also arise in inner source when contributors are able to finish their assigned work more quickly. Developers can also overcome their dependence on the maintainers of an inner source project as it allows them to fix defects or make changes themselves, very similar to open source projects.

In crowdsourcing, the community motivations are primarily extrinsic. On the TopCoder platform, various forms of remuneration (first and second prizes, reliability bonus, Digital Run funds) are available to active participants. Furthermore, the extrinsic motivation becomes even clearer given that many registered contestants will withdraw from competitions if they perceive that they have no chance of winning a prize. Also, some developers seek an official TopCoder rating and use that on their CVs to indicate independent validation of their technical ability. It thus forms a career signaling incentive similar to that proposed by Lerner and Tirole (2002).

5.1.4 Company Motivation

Motivations to adopt a 'traditional' outsourcing strategy include reduced development costs, reduced time-to-market as a result of 'follow-the-Sun' software development across multiple time-zones, cross-site modularization of development work, access to a larger and better skilled developer pool, innovation and shared best practices, and a closer proximity to customers (Ågerfalk and Fitzgerald 2006; Ó Conchúir et al. 2009).

A distinguishing motivation for opensourcing is that of commodification (Van der Linden et al. 2009). Increasingly, large parts of software systems are becoming 'commodities'—non-differentiating components that, although needed for a system to function properly, do not add any unique business value to a product. Classic examples are operating systems, database management systems and network protocol stacks (e.g., TCP/IP). No software company will, for example, implement their own database management system (unless, of course, their core product is a database systems). Another example is the DVTk-project discussed in Chap. 2. This project begun as a collaboration between Philips and AGFA because both companies felt that developing a proprietary toolkit would be wasting engineering resources that could be better spent on software that could lead to a competitive advantage. Moreover, the 'innovation happens elsewhere' argument appears to be a strong company incentive to engage in opensourcing since opensourcing allows companies to tap into a global developer community with competencies and experiences that the company may not have inhouse. Since open source developers are often also users, engaging with the community can also be a way of reaching out to, and even creating, new markets.

While innersourcing refers to the application of the open source development philosophy within an organization's boundaries, the motivations to adopt inner source differ significantly from those which are relevant to the adoption of opensourcing. Firstly, a key reason to adopt inner source is to increase internal reuse of software. By making available various internally developed software components to all departments, projects or business units, others can reuse these components as they see fit. Inner source can also help in reducing the time-to-market; Van der Linden et al. (2009) reported that Philips Healthcare was able to reduce the time-to-market by at least 3 months. Partly this faster shorter time-to-market will be a result of software reuse, but also due to the flexibility that the inner source model allows. Product divisions are empowered to make 'local' changes to the inner source product so as to allow them to overcome certain limitations (or to fix specific bugs) shortly before a product release, without escalating it to the 'core team' which may not have time to address these issues immediately.

Besides these motivations, 'open innovation' is another reason why a company may want to adopt inner source (Morgan et al. 2011). Similar to opensourcing, inner source projects can potentially attract a larger pool of developers (albeit within company boundaries) than found in conventional projects—especially in large, global organizations that employ thousands of people.

The motivation for companies who participate in crowdsourcing is certainly based on resource saving issues. Companies may be persuaded by the savings promised by crowdsourcing platforms—a 62 % saving suggested for software development using TopCoder, for example,[2] although the available evidence would

---

[2] http://techcrunch.com/2013/09/17/appirio-buys-topcoder-to-add-more-crowdsourcing-and-500k-developers-and-designers-to-its-cloudspokes-network/ (accessed 27 Sep 2014).

not appear to support this estimate (Stol and Fitzgerald 2014a). Also, they may not have in-house expertise in a particular topic or technology and seek to source that from the crowd. Also, the desire for innovation is certainly a factor as companies seek to get fresh thinking and ideas on topics. Indeed, this aspect is heavily promoted by the crowd platform providers.

5.1.5   Duration of Engagement

In traditional outsourcing the engagement tends to be project-specific as governed by a contract between both parties. Although a company may have a long-term relationship with a particular supplier, it will be episodic in so far as the contractual commitment will be as defined for each engagement.

While traditional outsourcing is primarily about commissioning software development to a third-party, opensourcing is rather about engaging in long-term collaborative activities that create and reinforce a sustainable ecosystem of individuals and organizations. Recently, Von Krogh et al. (2012) emphasized that although extrinsic motivation is important to sustainable community participation, long-term engagement and contribution to the community are even more critical.

Similar to opensourcing, the duration of engagement of developers in an inner source project tends to be long-term as developers will have a long-term interest in the software product. However, actual activity in terms of contributions, fixes, etc. can vary from daily activity to a very sporadic pattern, depending on the type of software as well as its level of maturity. For example, developers of the inner source project within Philips Research only worked on the project in 'bursts of activity' as defects or new requirements were identified (Stol and Fitzgerald 2015). Activity in this project would only last for a short time, after which weeks or months could pass before the next contributions. In contrast, other inner source projects can be in a state of perpetual development, similar to many large successful open source projects.

In crowdsourcing, the engagement between the company and community tends be to be short-term as defined by competitions, with ad hoc commitment from the community. Again, this is reflected in the "fleeting relationship" which characterises the crowdsourcing company community interaction. As already mentioned in Chap. 4, competitions of long duration tend not to be attractive to the crowd, and result in fewer and lower quality submissions. The recommendation from TopCoder is to have lots of competitions in parallel. Thus, the duration of engagement is geared much more towards a short-term model.

5.1.6   Nature of Participation

In the outsourcing context, the participation between customer and supplier is clearly collaborative. Suppliers are carefully chosen on the basis of their ability to perform a particular task. The company will decompose the work in such a way that the supplier will supply complementary offerings in a collaborative manner.

As noted above, the 'free rider' phenomenon has been identified as a threat to opensourcing. On a similar note, the ethics of crowdsourcing has been questioned due to its taking advantage of the creativity of the user community for commercial gains (Bruns 2007). Successful opensourcing, however, is characterized by reciprocity and symbiosis (cf. Dahlander and Magnusson 2005). In fact, in addition to individuals, the ecosystem that emerges in opensourcing is typically constituted by several commercial organizations that would normally compete but instead choose to collaborate on a particular project. Such collaboration between competitors is sometimes referred to as co-opetition.

The nature of participation in inner source projects is similar to opensourcing; participants in inner source projects are working collaboratively to improve the software. Again as in opensourcing, this collaboration may be implicit (everybody working towards a better product) or explicit (two or more developers working and discussing the implementation of a feature). They may work on a specific feature or module either on their own, or in collaboration with others while communicating through email or IRC.

In crowdsourcing, the nature of participation is clearly competitive. Crowd participants work on competitions in isolation without sharing or collaborating on solutions, and the best entry is adjudged to be the winner of the competition.

Interestingly, Brooks (1995) observed that software should be considered as public property and viewable to all. This is consistent with the open source model which has had enormous success due to the opportunities for learning that developers are afforded by being able to see the code of other developers. The nature of competition in crowdsourcing ensures that such sharing does not take place, and this is inevitably a sub-optimal situation.

5.2 Concluding Remarks

The outsourcing topic is not new and is one which has been thoroughly researched in the past. However, one of the key implications from our research is that the three alternative forms of open source inspired sourcing that we identify and discuss in this book differ both in significant and in subtle ways from the concept of outsourcing on a range of dimensions as illustrated in Table 5.1. Thus, we need to derive new concepts and rethink others to fully understand and leverage these alternate forms of sourcing.

In the literature, the terms offshoring and outsourcing are often used almost as synonyms. In keeping with Davis et al. (2004), however, it is possible to distinguish between the two:

- Offshoring is about location—when an activity is offshored it is performed in a different location to the main operation (which is then the onshore location).
- Outsourcing, on the other hand, is about governance—when an activity is outsourced it is performed by another organization, as opposed to 'in-house' by the organization itself.

Fig. 5.1 Shoring and
sourcing in the age of open

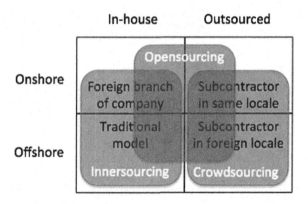

Consequently, the two concepts are orthogonal—an activity can be performed either offshore or onshore and can be performed in-house or be outsourced. Figure 5.1 shows the distinction and relationship between the two concepts and maps the three sourcing strategies discussed in this book onto the two concepts.

Interestingly, the global software engineering community has devoted considerable effort to distinguishing between different forms of 'shoring' based on location distance between collaborating sites using terms such as 'onshoring,' 'offshoring,' 'nearshoring' and 'farshoring' (Smite and Wohlin 2011). What becomes evident from our studies above is that in the age of open, distinguishing between forms of *shoring* has become a non-issue. Similarly what is in-house and what is subcontracted is no longer obvious. The nature of the unknown workforce means that it is not only irrelevant to talk about developer location, it is by definition *impossible*—any developer can be at any shore at any time (perhaps 'anyshoring' would be an appropriate term). Furthermore, while innersourcing is, per definition, in-house and crowdsourcing is a type of external subcontracting, opensourcing can happen both internally and internally in any given project. Thus, to understand software sourcing in the age of open, the important concept is no longer 'shoring' but rather the degree of 'workforce unknownness' and its implications for the development situation at hand.

References

Agarwal, R (2000) Individual Acceptance of Information Technologies, Framing The Domains of IT Management: Projecting the Future Through the Past, R. W. Zmud (ed.), Cincinnati, OH: Pinnaflex Press, pp. 85-104.

Ågerfalk, PJ (2013) Embracing diversity through mixed methods research, European Journal of Information Systems, Vol. 22, No. 3, pp. 251-256.

Ågerfalk, PJ (2015) Insufficient theoretical contribution: a conclusive rationale for rejection? European Journal of Information Systems, Vol 23, No 6, pp. 593–599.

Ågerfalk, PJ and Fitzgerald, B (2006) Flexible and Distributed Software Processes: Old Petunias in New Bowls? Communications of the ACM Vol. 49, No. 10, pp. 26-34

Ågerfalk, PJ and Fitzgerald, B (2008) Outsourcing to an Unknown Workforce: Exploring Opensourcing as a Global Sourcing Strategy, MIS Quarterly, Vol 32, No. 3, pp. 385–410

Asundi, J (2001) Software engineering lessons from open source projects. In Proceedings of the 1st Workshop on Open Source Software Engineering. J Feller, B Fitzgerald, and A van der Hoek (Eds.).

Asundi, J and Jayvant, R (2007) Patch review processes in open source software development communities: A comparative case study. In Proceedings of the 40th Annual Hawaii International Conference on Systems Sciences (HICSS).

Augustin, L, Bressler, D, and Smith, G (2002) Accelerating software development through collaboration. In Proceedings of the 24th International Conference on Software Engineering. pp. 559-563.

Aurum, A, Jeffery, R, Wohlin, C and Handzic, M (2003) Managing Software Engineering Knowledge, Springer.

Baldwin, CY and Clark, KB (2006) The architecture of participation: Does code architecture mitigate free riding in the open source development model? Management Science Vol. 52, No. 7, pp. 1116-1127.

Beecham, S, Baddoo, N, Hall, T, Robinson, H and Sharp, H (2008) Motivation in Software Engineering: A systematic literature review, Information and Software Technology, Vol. 50, No. 9-10.

Begel, A, Herbsleb, JD and Storey, MA (2012) The Future of Collaborative Software Development. In Proceedings of the ACM Conference on Computer Supported Cooperative Work (CSCW). ACM

Benkler, Y (2002) Coase's Penguin, or, Linux and the Nature of the Firm, The Yale Law Journal, Vol. 112, No. 3, pp. 369-446.

Bjørnson, FO and Dingsøyr, T (2008) Knowledge management in software engineering: A systematic review of studied concepts, findings and research methods used, Information and Software Technology, Vol. 50, No. 11.

Boehm, BW (1981) Software Engineering Economics, Pearson Education.

Boehm, B (2006) A View of 20th and 21st Century Software Engineering. In Proceedings of the International Conference on Software Engineering. Shanghai, China. ACM. pp. 12-29.

Bonabeau, E (2009) Decisions 2.0: The Power of Collective Intelligence, MIT Sloan Management Review, Vol. 50, No. 2, pp. 45-52.

Bonaccorsi, A and Rossi, C (2003) Why open source software can succeed. Research Policy Vol. 32, No. 7, pp. 1243-1258.

Brabham, DC (2008) Crowdsourcing as a Model for Problem Solving: An Introduction and Cases, Convergence, Vol. 14, No. 1.

Brabham, DC (2012) The Myth of Amateur Crowds: A critical discourse analysis of crowdsourcing coverage. Information, Communication & Society Vol. 15 No. 3.

Brabham, DC (2013) Crowdsourcing, MIT Press.

Brandenburger, AM, and Nalebuff, BJ (1996) Co-Opetition: A Revolution Mindset That Combines Competition and Co-operation, New York: Doubleday.

Brooks, FP (1995) The Mythical Man-Month. Addison Wesley Longman, Inc.

Bruns, A (2007) Produsage: Towards a Broader Framework for User-Led Content Creation, Proceedings of the 6th ACM SIGCHI Conference on Creativity and Cognition, Washington, DC.

Capiluppi, A, Stol, K, and Boldyreff, C (2012) Commercial Stakeholders in the Evolution of Open Source Software, in: Hammouda et al., Proceedings of the 8th International IFIP WG2.13 Conference on Open Source Systems (OSS), IFIP Advances in Information and Communication Technology (AICT), vol. 378, pp. 178-200.

Carmel, E (1999) Global Teams: Collaborating Across Borders and Time Zones, Upper Saddle River, NJ: Prentice-Hall.

Carmel, E (2006) Building Your Information Systems from the Other Side of the World: How Infosys Manages Time Zone Differences, MISQ Executive Vol. 5, No. 1, pp. 43-53.

Carmel, E, and Agarwal, R (2001) Tactical Approaches for Alleviating Distance in Global Software Development, IEEE Software Vol. 18, No. 2, pp. 22-29.

Carmel, E, and Tjia, P (2005) Offshoring Information Technology: Sourcing and Outsourcing to a Global Workforce, Cambridge, NY: Cambridge University Press.

Chatterjee, D, Grewal, R, and Sambamurthy, V (2002) Shaping Up for E-Commerce: Institutional Enablers of the Organizational Assimilation of Web Technologies, MIS Quarterly Vol. 26, No. 2, pp. 65-89.

Clary, EG, Snyder, M, Ridge, RD, Copeland, J, Stukas, AA, Haugen, J, Miene, P (1998) Understanding and Assessing the Motivations of Volunteers: A Functional Approach, Journal of Personality and Social Psychology, Vol. 74, No. 6, 1516–1530.

Crowston, K, Li, Q, Wei, K, Eseryel, UY, and Howison, J (2007) Self-organization of teams for free/libre open source software development. Inf. Softw. Technology Vol. 49, No. 6, pp. 564-575.

Dabbish, L, Farzan, R, Kraut, R and Postmes, T (2012) Fresh Faces in the Crowd: Turnover, Identity, and Commitment in Online Groups. In Proceedings of the ACM Conference on Computer-Supported Cooperative Work (CSCW). ACM.

Dahlander, L and Magnusson, MG (2005) Relationships between Open Source Software Companies and Communities: Observations from Nordic Firms, Research Policy (34), pp. 481–493.

Davis, GB, Ein-Dor, P, King, WR and Torkzadeh, R (2004) Information Technology Offshoring: Prospects, Challenges, Educational Requirements, and Curriculum Implications. Proceedings of the 25th International Conference on Information Systems, R. Agarwal, L.J. Kirsch, and J.I. DeGross (eds.), Washington, DC, December, pp. 1027–1038.

Dempsey, B, Weiss, D, Jones, P, and Greenberg, J (2002) Who Is an Open Source Software Developer?, Communications of the ACM Vol. 45, No. 2, pp. 67-72.

Dinh-Trong, T, and Bieman, JM (2004) Open Source Software Development: A Case Study of FreeBSD, in Proceedings of the 10th International Symposium on Software Metrics, IEEE Computer Society.

Dinkelacker, J, Garg, PK, Miller, R and Nelson, D (2002) Progressive open source. In Proceedings of the 24th International Conference on Software Engineering. pp. 177-184.

Doan, A, Ramakrishnan, R and Halevy, AY (2011) Crowdsourcing systems on the World-Wide Web, Communications of the ACM, Vol. 54, No. 4.

Dow, SP, Kulkarni, A, Klemmer, SR and Hartmann, B (2012) Shepherding the Crowd Yields Better Work. In Proceedings of the ACM Conference on Computer-Supported Cooperative Work (CSCW). ACM.

Ebert, C and De Neve, P (2001) Surviving Global Software Development. IEEE Software, Vol. 18, No. 2, pp. 62–69.

Erdogmus, H (2009) A process that is not. IEEE Software Vol. 26, No. 6, pp. 4-7.

Erenkrantz, JR (2003) Release management within open source projects. In Proceedings of the 3rd Workshop on Open Source Software Engineering. Feller, J, Fitzgerald, B, Hissam, SA and Lakhani, KR (Eds.).

Erenkrantz, JR and Taylor, RN (2003) Supporting distributed and decentralized projects: Drawing lessons from the open source community. In Proceedings of the 1st Workshop on Open Source in an Industrial Context. Marc Sihling (Ed.).

Feller, J and Fitzgerald, B (2002) Understanding Open Source Software Development. Pearson Education Ltd.

Feller, J, Fitzgerald, B, Hissam, S, and Lakhani, K. (Eds) (2005) Perspectives on Free and Open Source Software, MIT Press, Cambridge, MA.

Feller, J, Finnegan, P, Fitzgerald, B and Hayes, J (2008) From Peer Production to Productization: A Study of Socially Enabled Business Exchanges in Open Source Service Networks, Information Systems Research, Vol. 19, No. 4.

Fichman, RG (2004) Going Beyond the Dominant Paradigm for IT Innovation Research: Emerging Concepts and Methods, Journal of the Association for Information Systems Vol. 5, No. 8, pp. 314-355.

Fitzgerald, B (2006) The Transformation of Open Source Software, MIS Quarterly Vol. 30, No. 3, pp. 587-598.

Fitzgerald, B (2011) Open source software: Lessons from and for software engineering. IEEE Computer Vol. 44, No. 10, pp. 25-30.

Fitzgerald, B, Stol, K, O'Sullivan, R and O'Brien, D (2013) Scaling Agile Methods to Regulated Environments: An Industry Case Study. In Proceedings of the 35th International Conference on Software Engineering. San Francisco, CA, USA. IEEE.

Fogel, K (2005) Producing Open Source Software: How to Run a Successful Free Software Project. O'Reilly Media.

Gacek, C and Arief, B (2004) The many meanings of open source. IEEE Software Vol. 21, No. 1, pp. 34-40.

Gallivan, M (2001) Organizational Adoption and Assimilation of Complex Technological Innovations: Development and Application of a New Framework, The DATA BASE for Advances in Information Systems Vol. 32, No. 3, pp. 51-85.

Garvin, D (1993) Building a Learning Organization. Harvard Business Review Vol. 71, No. 4, pp. 78-91.

Gaughan, G, Fitzgerald, B, and Shaikh, M (2009) An examination of the use of open source software processes as a global software development solution for commercial software engineering. In Proceedings of the 35th Euromicro Conference on Software Engineering and Advanced Applications (SEAA), pp. 20-27.

German, DM (2005) Software Engineering Practices in the GNOME Project. In Perspectives on Free and Open Source Software, Feller, J., Fitzgerald, B, Hissam, SA, Lakhani, KR (Eds.) MIT Press

Ghosh, RA (2005) Understanding Free Software Developers: Findings from the FLOSS Study, in Perspectives on Free and Open Source Software, Feller, J., Fitzgerald, B, Hissam, SA, Lakhani, KR (Eds.) MIT Press

Goldman, R, and Gabriel, RP (2005) Innovation Happens Elsewhere: Open Source as Business Strategy, San Francisco: Morgan Kauffman Publishers.

Gonzalez, R, Gasco, J and Llopis, J (2006) Information Systems Outsourcing: A literature analysis, Information & Management Vol. 43, No. 7, pp. 821-834.

Gorman, M (2004) Understanding The Linux Virtual Memory Manager, Technical Report, University of Limerick, Ireland.

Greengard, S (2011) Following the Crowd, Communications of the ACM Vol. 54, No. 2, pp. 20-22.

Gurbani, VK, Garvert, A and Herbsleb, JD (2006) A case study of a corporate open source development model. In Proceedings of the 28th International Conference on Software Engineering. pp. 472-481.

Gurbani, VK, Garvert, A and Herbsleb, JD (2010) Managing a corporate open source software asset. Communications of the ACM Vol. 53, No. 2, pp. 155-159.

Halloran, TJ and Scherlis, WL (2002) High quality and open source software practices. In Proceedings of the 2nd Workshop on Open Source Software Engineering. Feller, J, Fitzgerald, B, Hecker, F, Hissam, SA, Lakhani, K and van der Hoek, A (Eds.).

Herbsleb, JD, and Grinter, RE (1999) Splitting the Organization and Integrating the Code: Conway's Law Revisited, in Proceedings of the 21st International Conference on Software Engineering, Los Angeles, California.

Herbsleb, JD and Mockus, A (2003) An Empirical Study of Speed and Communication in Globally Distributed Software Development, IEEE Transactions on Software Engineering, Vol. 29, No. 6.

Hoffmann, L (2009) Crowd Control, Communications of the ACM, Vol. 52, No. 3.

Höst, M, Stol, K, and Oručević-Alagic, A (2014) Inner Source Project Management, to appear in Software Project Management in a Changing World, Ruhe G and Wohlin C (Eds.), Springer.

Howe, J (2008) Crowdsourcing: Why the Power of the Crowd Is Driving the Future of Business, Crown Business.

Inkpen, AC (1996) Creating Knowledge through Collaboration, California Management Review Vol. 39, No. 1, pp. 123-140.

Ipeirotis, PG (2010) Analyzing the Amazon Mechanical Turk marketplace, XRDS, Vol. 17, No. 2, pp. 16-21.

Ipeirotis, PG and Paritosh, PK (2011) Managing Crowdsourced Human Computation. In Proceedings WWW.

Jørgensen, N (2005) Incremental and Decentralized Integration in FreeBSD. in Perspectives on Free and Open Source Software, J. Feller B. Fitzgerald, S. Hissam, and K. Lakhani (eds.), Cambridge, MA: MIT Press

Kazman, R and Chen, HM (2009) The Metropolis Model: A new Logic for Development of crowdsourced systems, Communications of the ACM, Vol. 52, No. 7.

Kinnaird, P, Dabbish, L, Kiesler, S and Faste, H (2013) Co-Worker Transparency in a Microtask Marketplace. In Proceedings Computer Supported Coordination Work.

Kittur, A (2010) Crowdsourcing, Collaboration and Creativity, XRDS, Vol. 17, No. 2.

Kittur, A, Smus, B, Khamkar, S and Kraut, RE (2011) CrowdForge: Crowdsourcing Complex Work. In Proceedings of the ACM Symposium on User Interface Software and Technology.

Kittur, A, Nickerson, JV, Bernstein, MS, Gerber, EM, Shaw, A, Zimmerman, J, Lease, M and Horton, JJ (2013) The Future of Crowd Work. In Proceedings of the ACM Conference on Computer-Supported Cooperative Work (CSCW). ACM.

Koh, C, Ang, S, and Straub, DW (2004) IT Outsourcing Success: A Psychological Contract Perspective, Information Systems Research Vol. 15, No. 4, pp. 356-373.

Kraut, RE and Streeter, LA (1995) Coordination in Software Development, Communications of the ACM, Vol. 38, No. 3.

Kulkarni, A, Can, M and Hartmann, B (2012) Collaboratively Crowdsourcing Workflows with Turkomatic. In Proceedings of the ACM Conference on Computer-Supported Cooperative Work (CSCW). ACM.

Lacity, M, Khan, S, Yan, A, and Willcocks, L (2010) A Review of the IT Outsourcing Empirical Literature and Future Research Directions, Journal of Information Technology, Vol. 25, No. 4, pp. 395-433.

Lakhani, KR and Panetta, JA (2007) The Principles of Distributed Innovation, Innovations: Technology, Governance, Globalization, Vol. 2, No. 3.

Lakhani, KR, and Wolf, RG (2005) Why Hackers Do What They Do: Understanding Motivation and Effort in Free/Open Source Software Projects. in Perspectives on Free and Open Source Software, J. Feller B. Fitzgerald, S. Hissam, and K. Lakhani (eds.), Cambridge, MA: MIT Press

Lakhani, KR, Garvin, DA and Lonstein, E (2010) TopCoder (A): Developing Software through Crowdsourcing, Harvard Business School 610-032.

LaToza, TD, Towne, WB, van der Hoek, A and Herbsleb, JD (2013) Crowd Development. In Proceedings of the 6th CHASE Workshop. San Francisco, CA, USA. IEEE.

Leonard-Barton, D (1995) Wellsprings of Knowledge: Building and Sustaining the Sources of Innovation, Boston: Harvard Business School Press.

Lerner, J, and Tirole, J (2002) Some Simple Economics of Open Source, The Journal of Industrial Economics Vol. 50, No. 2, pp. 197-234.

Lings B, Lundell B, Ågerfalk P J, Fitzgerald B (2007) A reference model for successful Distributed Development of Software Systems. Proceedings of the 2nd International Conference on Global Software Engineering (ICGSE 2007), Munich, Germany, 27–30 August 2007.

MacCormack, A, Rusnak, J and Baldwin, CY (2006) Exploring the structure of complex software designs: An empirical study of open source and proprietary code. Management Science Vol. 52, No. 7, pp. 1015-1030.

Malone, TW and Crowston, K (1994) The Interdisciplinary Study of Coordination, ACM Computing Surveys, Vol 26, No. 1.

McConnell, SC (1999) Open-source methodology: Ready for prime time? IEEE Software Vol. 16, No. 4, pp. 6-8.

Melian, C (2007) Progressive open source. Ph.D. Dissertation. Stockholm School of Economics, Sweden.

Merilinna, J and Matinlassi, M (2006) State of the art and practice of open source component integration. In Proceedings of the 32nd Euromicro Conference on Software Engineering and Advanced Applications (SEAA) pp. 170-177.

Michlmayr, M and Fitzgerald, B (2012) Time-based release management in free and open source (FOSS) projects. International Journal of Open Source Software and Processes Vol. 4, No. 1, pp. 1-19.

Michlmayr, M, Fitzgerald, B, Stol, K (2015) Why and How Should Open Source Projects Adopt Time-Based Releases? IEEE Software, Vol. 32, No. 2.

Millar, C, Choi, CJ, Russell, ET, and Kim, JB (2005) Open Source Communities: An Integrally Informed Approach, Journal of Organizational Change Management Vol. 18, No. 3, pp. 259-268.

Mockus, A and Herbsleb, JD (2002) Why Not Improve Coordination in Distributed Software Development by Stealing Good Ideas from Open Source?, in Meeting Challenges and Surviving Success: The Second Workshop on Open Source Software Engineering, pp. 19-25.

Mockus, A, Fielding, RT, and Herbsleb, JD (2002) Two Case Studies of Open Source Software Development: Apache and Mozilla, ACM Transactions on Software Engineering and Methodology Vol. 11, No. 3, pp. 309-346.

Morgan, L, Feller, J, and Finnegan, P (2011) Exploring inner source as a form of intraorganisational open innovation. Proceedings of the European Conference on Information Systems, Helsinki, Finland.

Moore, G (1999) Crossing the Chasm, Harper, NY

Nakatsu, RT and Iacovou, CL (2009) A Comparative Study of Important Risk Factors Involved in Offshore and Domestic Outsourcing of Software Development Projects: A Two-Panel Delphi Study, Information & Management Vol. 46, No. 1, pp 57-68.

Neus, A and Scherf, P (2005) Opening minds: cultural change with the introduction of open source collaboration methods. IBM Systems Journal Vol. 44, No. 2, pp. 215-225.

Nonaka, I (1991) The Knowledge-Creating Company, Harvard Business Review (69:6), pp. 96-104.

Nov, O (2007) What motivates wikipedians? Communications of the ACM, 50(11), 60-64.

Ó Conchúir, E, Ågerfalk, PJ, Holmström Olsson H, and Fitzgerald, B (2009) Global software development: never mind the problems—where are the benefits? Communications of the ACM, Vol 52, No 8.

O'Mahony, S (2005) Non-Profit Foundations and Their Role in Community-Firm Software Collaboration, in Perspectives on Free and Open Source Software, J. Feller B. Fitzgerald, S. Hissam, and K. Lakhani (eds.), Cambridge, MA: MIT Press, pp. 393-414.

O'Reilly, T (1999) Lessons from open source software development. Communications of the ACM Vol. 42, No. 4, pp. 33-37

Parnas, DL (1972) On the criteria to be used in decomposing systems into modules. Communications of the ACM Vol. 15, No. 12, pp. 1053-1058.

Raymond, ES (2001) The Cathedral & the Bazaar: Musings on Linux and Open Source by an Accidental Revolutionary. O'Reilly Media.

Riehle, D, Ellenberger, J, Menahem, T, Mikhailovski, B, Natchetoi, Y, Naveh, B and Odenwald, T (2009) Open collaboration within corporations using software forges. IEEE Software Vol. 26, No. 2, pp. 52-58.

Riehle, D, Riemer, P, Kolassa, C, and Schmidt, M (2014) Paid vs. Volunteer Work in Open Source. In Proceedings of the 47th Hawaii International Conference on System Science. pp. 3286-3295.

Riemens, B and van Zon, K (2006) PFSPD short history. http://pfspd.sourceforge.net/history.html.

Rigby, PC, German, DM and Storey, MA (2008) Open source software peer review practices: A case study of the Apache Server. In Proceedings of the 30th International Conference on Software Engineering. ACM, pp. 541-550.

Rigby, PC, Cleary, B, Painchaud, F, Storey, MA and German, DM (2012) Contemporary peer review in action: Lessons from open source development. IEEE Software Vol. 29, No. 6. pp. 56-61.

Robbins, J (2005) Adopting open source software engineering (OSSE) practices by adopting OSSE tools. In Perspectives on Free and Open Source Software, Feller, J, Fitzgerald, B, Hissam, SA, and Lakhani, KR (Eds.), MIT Press, pp. 245-264.

Robles, G, Scheider, H, Tretkowski, I, and Weber, N (2001) Who is doing it? A research on libre software developers. *Research Paper, TU Berlin, August.*

Royce, WW (1987) Managing the development of large software systems. In Proceedings of the 9th International Conference on Software Engineering. Originally published in Proceedings of WESCON'70. pp. 328-338.

Scacchi, W (2002) Understanding the Requirements for Developing Open Source Software Systems, IEE Proceedings—Software Vol. 149, No. 1, pp. 24-39.

Scacchi, W (2004) Free and open source development practices in the game community. IEEE Software Vol. 21, No. 1, pp. 59-66.

Schenk, E and Guittard, C (2011) Towards a Characterization of Crowdsourcing Practices, Journal of Innovation Economics, Vol. 1, No. 7.

Senyard, A and Michlmayr, M (2004) How to have a successful free software project. In Proceedings of the 11th Asia-Pacific Software Engineering Conference (APSEC).

Smite, D and Wohlin, C (2011) A whisper of evidence in global software engineering, IEEE Software, Vol. 28, No. 4, pp. 15-18

Stol, K and Fitzgerald, B (2014a) Two's Company, Three's a Crowd: A Case Study of Crowdsourcing Software Development, International Conference on Software Engineering, Hyderabad, India, May 2014, pp. 187–198.

Stol, K and Fitzgerald, B (2014b) Researching Crowdsourcing Software Development: Perspectives and Concerns. In Proceedings of the First International Workshop on Crowdsourcing in Software Engineering (CSI-SE) co-located with ICSE'14, Hyderabad, India

Stol, K and Fitzgerald B (2014c) Research Protocol for a Case Study of Crowdsourcing Software Development. Technical Report. University of Limerick.

Stol, K and Fitzgerald, B (2015) Inner Source—Adopting Open Source Development Practices within Organizations: A Tutorial, IEEE Software, Vol. 32.

Stol, K, Babar, MA, Avgeriou, P and Fitzgerald, B (2011) A comparative study of challenges in integrating open source software and inner source software. Information and Software Technology Vol. 53, No. 12, pp. 1319-1336.

Stol, K, Avgeriou, P, Babar, M, Lucas, Y and Fitzgerald, B (2014) Key Factors for Adopting Inner Source, ACM Transactions on Software Engineering Methodology (TOSEM), Vol. 23, No. 2

Surowiecki, J (2005) The Wisdom of Crowds: Why the Many Are Smarter Than the Few, Abacus.

Tajedin, H and Nevo, D (2013) Determinants of success in crowdsourcing software development. In Proceedings of SIGMIS Computer and People Research. Cincinnati, OH, USA.

Tiwana, A and Keil, M (2009) Control in Internal and Outsourced Software Projects, Journal of Management Information Systems (26:3), pp 9-44.

Torkar, R, Minoves, P and Garrigos, J (2011) Adopting free/libre/open source software practices, techniques and methods for industrial use. Journal of the Association of Information Systems Vol. 12, No. 1, pp. 88-122.

Torvalds, L (1999) The Linux edge. In Open Sources: Voices from the Open Source Revolution, Chris DiBona, Sam Ockman, and Mark Stone (Eds.), O'Reilly Media.

Torvalds, L (2000) Linux Kernel mailing list. https://lkml.org/lkml/2000/8/25/132.

Van der Linden, F, Schmid, K and Rommes, E (2007) Software Product Lines in Action: The Best Industrial Practice in Product Line Engineering. Springer.

Van der Linden, F, Lundell, B and Marttiin, P (2009) Commodification of industrial software: A case for open source. IEEE Software, Vol. 26, No. 4, pp. 77-83.

Venkatesh, V, Brown, S A, and Bala H (2013) Bridging the qualitative–quantitative divide: guidelines for conducting mixed methods research in information systems. MIS Quarterly 36(1), 21-54.

Vitharana, P, King, J and Chapman, HS (2010) Impact of internal open source development on reuse: Participatory reuse in action. Journal of Management Information Systems Vol. 27, No. 2, pp. 277-304.

Von Hippel, E, and Von Krogh, G (2003) Open Source Software and the 'Private-Collective' Innovation Model: Issues for Organization Science, Organization Science Vol. 14, No. 2, pp. 209-223.

Von Krogh, G., Haefliger, S., Spaeth, S, and Wallin, M. W. (2012) Carrots and Rainbows: Motivation and Social Practice in Open Source Software Development. MIS Quarterly, Vol. 36, No. 2, pp. 649-676.

Vukovic, M (2009) Crowdsourcing for Enterprises. SERVICES.

Wesselius, J (2008) The bazaar inside the cathedral: Business models for internal markets. IEEE Software, Vol. 25, No. 3, pp. 60-66.

Wheeler, D (2004) Why Open Source Software/Free Software (OSS/FS, FLOSS, or FOSS)? Look at the Numbers!, available online at http://www.dwheeler.com/oss_fs_why.html.

Zhao, Y and Zhu, Q (2012) Evaluation on crowdsourcing research: Current status and future direction, Information Systems Frontiers, April.

Printed in the United States
By Bookmasters